Unbullyable:
Bullying solutions for parents and children

The sensational new approach

Sue Anderson

First published and distributed in Australia
in 2013 by Good2gr8 Coaching

Unbullyable ®
Copyright © 2013 by Sue Anderson

The right of Sue Anderson to be identified as the
author of this work has been asserted by her in accordance with the
Copyright Amendment (Moral Rights) Act 2000.

All rights reserved. No part of this book may be
reproduced by any mechanical, photographic, or electrical process,
or in the form of a phonographic recording; nor may it be stored in a
retrieval system, transmitted, or otherwise copied for public or private,
use – other than for 'fair use' as brief quotations embodied in articles
and reviews – without prior written permission of the author.

ISBN: 978-0-9875609-0-2
A Cataloging in Publication entry is available from
the National Library of Australia.

Content: Sue Anderson
Editor: Glenda Downing
Illustrator: Lucinda Hateley
Designer: Pageset
Typesetter: Pageset
Front cover design: Danijela Mijailović
Printed in Australia by McPherson's Printing Group
Contact: www.unbullyable.com.au or info@unbullyable.com.au

The material contained in this publication is
of the nature of general comment only and is not
intended to advise on any particular matter.
Readers should not act on the basis of any material in the publication
without obtaining advice relevant to their own particular situation.
The author/editor and publisher expressly disclaim any liability to any
person in respect of any action taken or not taken
in reliance on the contents of this publication.

What to do if your child is not coping with being bullied

*I'd like to make it very clear from the
beginning of this book that if you discover your
child is experiencing suicidal thoughts or self-harming,
seek **immediate professional help**. Take action NOW – don't
wait to see if things work themselves out.
Sadly, children as young as eleven years of age have taken
their lives because of bullying. It's just not worth
risking the life of your beautiful child.*

Contents

	Preface	9
	Acknowledgements	11
	Introduction	13
1	The bullying experience	19
2	Exploring your beliefs about bullying	35
3	Changing your beliefs about bullying	51
4	Your child's beliefs about bullying	65
5	Conversations about bullying	75
6	Self-esteem inside out	97
7	The power to choose	123
8	An *Unbullyable* state	141
9	Empowering emotions	157
10	*Unbullyable* movies	181
11	*Unbullyable* thinking styles	203
12	Cyberbullying	221
13	Bullies	237
	Afterword	253
	Resources and websites	255
	Notes	257
	Bibliography and references	261
	Index	263
	About the author	272

Preface

Welcome to the journey of supporting your child move from bullied to *Unbullyable*.

My goal is to facilitate ONE MILLION people move from bullied to *Unbullyable*, and I would love it if your child could be one of those people. As a parent of three gorgeous, beautiful, precious children (I'm just a little biased!), I know what it is to want my children to be happy. And when children are bullied, they are far from happy. I am motivated to help by the fact that, every night, there are children all over the world who cry themselves to sleep because they are the targets of bullying. Sadly, some of these children find it too much to endure, can see no end to their pain, and take their own life. Yet I know it doesn't have to be this way, because parents *can* help. There *is* something we can do about bullying.

This book has been seven years in the thinking and three years in the writing. In these pages I share with you everything I know about helping children move from bullied to *Unbullyable*. I have also written this book in support of you, your child's parent. The theory is based on what I have learnt and applied in my studies of psychology, cognitive behaviour sciences, Neuro-Linguistic Programming (NLP), Neuro-Semantics (NS) and Meta-Coaching. Yet writing this book has required more than just knowledge of theory. I have used my years of specialising in coaching children affected by bullying to write this book in support of you. I want you to know what I know, so you can help your child. I want you to be able to answer the question I'm asked by parents on a daily basis: *'How can I help my bullied child?'*

I started coaching children affected by bullying in 2006. I didn't set out to be the 'Bullying Lady', as some people call me. It has just magically turned out that way – and I'm so glad. I'm privileged to have amazingly powerful conversations about bullying every day. I get to coach, train, write and present (yes I even enjoy public speaking because it means I'm spreading the message), 'We CAN do something about bullying. It's not all doom and gloom.' Some people ask me if it's depressing working with bullied children every day. I tell them it's the opposite. It's inspiring, uplifting and empowering to work with children who have had enough and who are keen to move from bullied to *Unbullyable*.

Acknowledgements

Thanks to these special souls: my amazing, charismatic husband Chris Cartledge, who introduced me to the wonders of coaching, and who continues to inspire me. My beautiful treasures, Cleo (Sissy), Jarvy and Jaz: you are my everything. To my beautiful mother-in-law, Annie Cartledge, who looked after my children for many hours so I could write. To Michelle Duval, my mentor, whose generosity overwhelms me. To all the ECMers: your support has been incredible. To my family and friends who put up with my years of constant 'book talk' and who would ask me 'How's your book going?', your support has been amazing. Thank you to Natalie Squire, Julia Selkirk, Marea Campbell, Margaret Anderson, Greg Whitecross, Leanne Baxter, Rana Stollery, John and Jayne Campbell, Sylvie Homes, Joanne Campbell, Alison Lisle, Pina Worsley, Des Lowe, Dina Cooper, Marija Castellari, Lucinda Hateley, Kylee and Jeff Ellerton, John and Jacqui, Helen Stephens, Kay Jackson, Lisa Young, Josette Wunder, Yvette Hughes, Sally Grimwood and to all the random strangers I struck up conversations with who were happy to share their stories with me.

To the great mind, Dr L. Michael Hall, who continues to contribute to the betterment of the human race through his ongoing development of Neuro-Semantics. Michael took the time to read my draft manuscripts to ensure this book reflects the basis of Neuro-Semantics. While this book is based mainly on Neuro-Semantics, it also builds on, but is not limited to, the work of many creative minds, including Bob Bodenhamer, Richard Bandler, John Grinder, Alfred Korzybski, Robert Dilts, Michelle Duval, Lucus Derks, Judith DeLozier, Aaron Beck and Albert Ellis.

And finally, to the hundreds of children, teenagers, parents, grandparents and teachers who were brave enough to share their bullying experiences with me. I thank you and am truly honoured. You are my inspiration.

Introduction

Do you remember looking at your newborn baby in her first few minutes of life? Her face all blotchy and squishy. Maybe as you looked in wonder at your precious bundle you thought to yourself, *'I'm never going to let anyone hurt you.'* I know I did.

Most of us feel that strong protective urge of parenting. We consider it our role to keep our babies safe, and nurture them to grow into happy, confident children who love life. We send them off to school with the hope they will enjoy it, develop a love of learning, make friends and love themselves. Our child being bullied is definitely not in the plan we map out for them.

Yet for many parents, their child being bullied becomes a reality. The statistics are frightening. According to Australian research, one in four children are bullied frequently (every few weeks or more often).[1] Many parents are faced with the harsh reality that someone *is* hurting their child and want to help, but sometimes they don't know how to help, or what to do. *'This is not what I signed up for. This is not meant to be happening to my child!'*

With the rates of bullying high among children, some parents are beginning to wonder if bullying is becoming a normal part of growing up. Is it human nature that some children who are considered a little different, shy or 'loners' are picked on, singled out and abused by children considered more popular, confident or powerful? Has it become an expectation that a percentage of our children are bullied? As time goes on, will we accept bullying as a normal part of growing up?

I hope not. Let's do something about it.

NOW.

Most parents I talk with are horrified at the amount of bullying among children and would love to do something about it. But they're not sure what to do, or how to make a difference.

Sadly, however, a small percentage of parents believe being the target of bullying is normal, or even 'character building'. I call it the 'suck it up, princess' approach to bullying. I have been shocked at the attitudes some parents have towards bullying. When I shared with one mum that I coach bullied children to become Unbullyable, she turned to me and said: '*I was bullied as a girl and I used it as motivation to do well at school. I turned out okay. It's just part of human nature. The fact is, there has always been bullying and always will be. Kids these days are too soft. They need to toughen up a bit and get over themselves.*'

Hmm. Some parents might argue children need to pour themselves a cup of concrete and harden up, but that attitude is almost like accepting it. Isn't that like saying, 'Well, there's really nothing you can do about it love, so just put up with it?' Should parents cross their fingers and hope their child has the ability to toughen up and get over it? And what if they don't? What then?

Our children deserve better than that.

What is different about the *Unbullyable* approach?

Most books on bullying work from a definition based on the behaviours of the bully. These definitions fail to consider that, in every case, the way the target of the bullying *thinks* about the bully has a powerful effect on the impact of the bullying. What I offer you is a new way of thinking about bullying and, importantly, how to make that change in your thinking. Together, we explore how your child can choose to change the way she thinks about bullying, and herself as a target of bullying. (Throughout this book I call the child the bullying behaviour is directed towards the 'target', rather than the 'victim'. Targets can move. Targets can be missed. The bullying behaviour does not always hit its target.)

As you may know from first-hand experience, much advice about how to help your child is limited in its effectiveness. The reason it is limited is because it focuses on telling your child to change her behaviour only, and ignores your child's thinking. In fact, many well-intentioned parents tell their child to change her behaviour (for example, by saying 'just ignore them'), only to end up feeling *more* helpless because the advice does not help their child. In addition, some children try these strategies once or twice without success, and simply give up trying. They are then in danger of thinking there is nothing they can do about being bullied, and incorrectly conclude they are powerless. Your child is not powerless, helpless or hopeless. This book outlines how you can help your child to choose to be empowered.

What can you do?

There are many ways you can help your child. If your child is currently being bullied, or you believe she is in danger of being bullied, and you would like to help her become *Unbullyable*, this book is for you. In the following pages I show you how to encourage your child to empower herself, and also to empower yourself as a parent of a bullied child.

Many parents give themselves a hard time about their child being bullied and become paralysed by feelings of helplessness, anger, disempowerment, guilt or frustration. I spend hours reassuring parents that their child being the target of bullying *is not their fault*. It is *not* a reflection of their parenting skills. They have *not* failed their child. If parents are blaming themselves, and getting bogged down with negative, disempowering emotions, they are not in a position to help their child. I invite and support you to explore your beliefs, your emotions and your thinking about bullying so that you are in the best position possible to empower your child. Does that sound like something you would like?

Imagine the difference to the quality of your child's life if she considers herself *Unbullyable*. Imagine how differently your child will experience the world when she knows that while other children might *try* to bully her, it won't work because she *chooses how she thinks and feels*. Imagine helping your child know she can choose how she responds to other people's attempts to bully her.

If that was true for you:
- How would you think and believe about bullying?
- What would your child being *Unbullyable* mean to you? To your child? To your family?
- How would you let your child know she can choose to be unaffected by other people's attempts to bully her?

A different approach that actually works

Let's focus on the most crucial aspect of the bullying experience: *meaning and beliefs*. How your child thinks about bullying has the greatest impact on her bullying experience.

What your child believes about bullying is far more important than any 'behavioural strategies' other bullying books offer. *Unbullyable* offers you a new and different way to think about bullying. There are step-by-step processes to follow to help your child. Read real stories of real families affected by bullying, and how they moved from bullied to *Unbullyable*.

I invite you to take from this book what works and suits your family. I offer you a unique, tried-and-true approach I know works. Say goodbye to not knowing what to say or do to help your child and see for yourself how you can help that squishy little bundle of joy be the happy, confident, and *Unbullyable* child you dreamed for.

1

The bullying experience

If, like me, you are a busy parent, you might be tempted to think, *'Oh, just hurry up and tell me what page the solution is on.'* If only it were that easy! Through working with bullied children and their parents, I know from experience that the parents who helped their child the most successfully are the ones who have taken the time to educate themselves, and have firstly explored their own thinking and feelings about bullying. If you want to help your child, and are committed to the process, I encourage you to give yourself the time and space you need to read and absorb the information in this chapter.

Let's explore the following questions:
- What is bullying?
- Why define bullying in a new way?
- How do children define bullying?
- How bullyable is your child?
- What clues may indicate your child is being bullied?

What is bullying?
Who decides when playful teasing becomes bullying? Is it the target, the bully, the teachers, or the parents? And what criteria are

used to make that decision? How can we define bullying in a way that gives us a clear answer? Most common definitions of bullying are based on the behaviours of the bully. These definitions ignore the fact that the way the target of the bullying *thinks* has a huge effect on the impact of the bullying. I'm inviting you to consider bullying in a different way. Let's pull apart the commonly used definition of bullying and look at it with different eyes.

The following is an example of a definition of bullying from the 2011 *Australian National Safe Schools Framework Resource Manual:*[2]

Bullying is a pattern of repeated physical, verbal, psychological or social aggression that is directed towards a specific student by someone with more power and is intended to cause harm, distress and/or create fear.

Most definitions of bullying have these four components:
1. Intention to cause harm
2. Repeated
3. By one individual or a group against another individual or group
4. Power imbalance

Let's explore these four components in detail to clarify exactly what bullying is, and what it is not.

1. Intention to cause harm
Most definitions of bullying state the bully has the *intention* to cause harm to your child. But this is a mind read, an assumption, and we never truly know the intentions of a bully. (We explore reasons why a bully bullies in more detail in Chapter Thirteen.)

As a coach who works with bullies, I agree that in most cases the purpose of a bully's actions is to deliberately harm others. Bullies achieve this socially (by isolation), psychologically (by intimidation), or physically (by physical contact). This component of the definition requires that the purpose, intention and goal of the bully's behaviour is premeditated. A child accidentally knocking your child over is not bullying, but a child planning and then carrying out the action of throwing your child's school bag on the canteen roof every morning to try to cause your child anxiety and annoyance could be considered bullying (if the behaviour is also repeated and directed at your child).

2. Repeated

For behaviour to be considered bullying, it must be an ongoing pattern of behaviour. We are not talking about a one-off incident that grew out of control. We are not talking about a fight between two children who usually do not fight. We're talking about a series of interactions, which are repeated and occur over a period of time. The length of time may vary from days or weeks to *years*. A child making a joke about another child's appearance once is not bullying, even though the recipient of the 'joke' may be very upset. A child making cruel or racist statements about another child's appearance most days over a period of six months could be considered bullying (if the behaviour is intended to cause harm and is directed at your child).

3. By one individual or a group against another individual or group

Bullying occurs within relationships. If there is no interaction between the bully and the target, the bullying cannot occur. The bully needs someone to project the bullying behaviour on to. The bullying scenario could be one bully and one target, or numerous bullies and one target, or between groups of individuals. A child randomly yelling abuse and another child walking past and hearing it is not bullying. A child yelling abuse directed and targeted *at* a particular child could be considered bullying (if the behaviour is intended to cause harm and is repeated).

4. Power imbalance

As bullying occurs within a relationship, for it to be successful for the bully there needs to be a perceived power imbalance on both accounts. I say 'perceived' deliberately. The bully needs to believe they make *another* child feel scared, annoyed, intimidated or upset etc. And that child needs to believe the bully *makes* them feel scared, annoyed, intimidated or upset etc. This explains why some bullies are also bullied. They believe they make others feel a certain way – and they believe others make them feel a certain way. Your child can decide no one has power over them to 'make' them feel anything. Your child can learn how to choose what he thinks, believes and how he feels. We will fully explore the concept of power and how it relates to your child's bullying experience in Chapter Seven.

Let's take that common definition and expand it further by introducing two *new concepts* I believe are crucial to empowering your child in the bullying experience:
    5. Limiting beliefs and meanings
    6. Unresourceful states

5. Limiting beliefs and meanings

This is the first of the two 'new' components I believe are required for bullying to occur. What your child believes about himself is crucial in his bullying experience. If your child believes he can be bullied, he is bullyable – and he will most likely be bullied. If your child believes the bully can say whatever they want and it doesn't *mean* anything to him, the bullying will have less of an impact on him. The point here is that success or failure of the bullying attempt is ultimately determined by the meaning your child gives it.

> *The success or failure of the bullying attempt is ultimately determined by the meaning your child gives it.*

For behaviour to be truly successful from the bully's perspective, your child has to give it a negative meaning. The behaviour or comment has to *equal* something bad, or nasty, or be insulting to your child. Behaviours that may look insignificant to you or your child's teacher may be highly meaningful to your child. For example, a child tells his teacher: *'He keeps moving my bag to the end locker!'* (Everybody knows what that means! The end locker is where the losers put their bag…My bag in the end locker means I am a loser…) This example explains why a teacher can sincerely say to you, *'I was watching the whole time…I did not see your child being bullied.'* The bullying is 'hidden' or 'covert'.

Your child can learn to give the bully's behaviour a different meaning – one that is more resourceful.

6. Unresourceful states

The second of the new components I am introducing is 'state'. It is so powerful, yet ignored by other approaches to bullying. Your state refers to everything about how you are feeling. It's a combination of your state of mind, physical state, and emotional state. It could be your nervousness, your hunger, your sense of fun, your boredom or seriousness. You are always in a state.

Both your child and the child doing the bullying are in individual and unique 'states' when the bullying is taking place. The bullying works best for the bully when your child is in an unresourceful state – for example, a state of powerlessness, fear and hurt. The bully might step into a state of anger, insecurity or jealously and so on when they are attempting to bully your child.

It may not feel like it right now, but you can learn how you can choose the state you are in. As we will explore in Chapter Eight, your child can choose to powerfully move from an unresourceful state to a more resourceful state. In a resourceful state – for example, a state of curiosity, 'un-insult-ability' and powerfulness – the bullying attempts are much less successful. When your child realises he can choose the state he's in when the bully attempts to bully him, he is a step closer to becoming *Unbullyable*. Sounds good, doesn't it?

Why define bullying in a new way?

But wait, there's more! Not only am I including two new components to the bullying definition, I'm inviting you to see *your child's power* in the bullying experience, which I believe has been ignored up until now. As you read through the six components involved in bullying, you may notice the first three are influenced by the bully, and beyond the control of your child:

1. The *bully* (generally) intends to harm your child
2. The *bully* repeats the behaviour over time
3. The *bully's* behaviour is targeted at your child

THE BULLYING EXPERIENCE

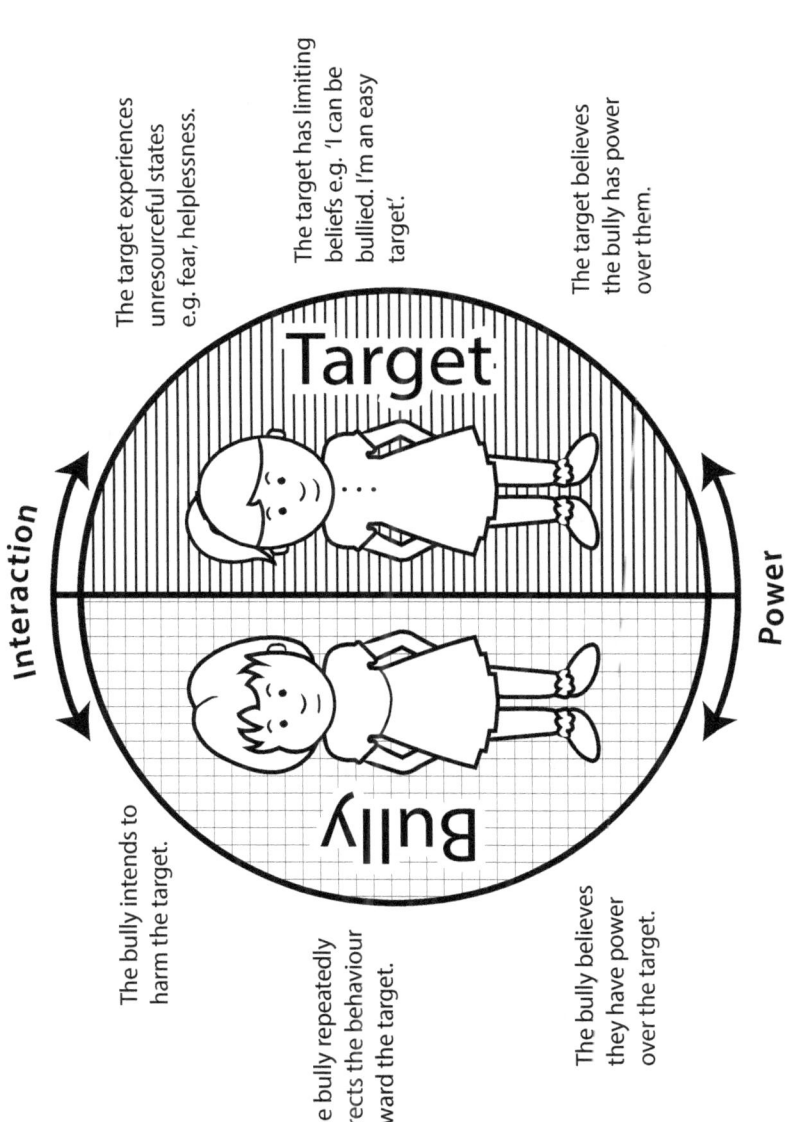

But, excitingly, the next three components can be influenced by *your child*:

4. *Your child* believes the bully has the power over him
5. *Your child* has limiting beliefs and unresourceful meanings
6. *Your child* is in an unresourceful state

Can you see how your child's thoughts about *power*, *beliefs* and *states* make up half of the bullying experience? In other words, instead of having no control over the bullying experience, your child has influence over three of the six components. Your child plays a very important and powerful role in the interaction, and has the ability to interrupt, cut short or stubbornly refuse to participate in another child's attempt to bully him.

These three components are the key to you helping your child. We explore each of these in detail in Chapters Four, Seven and Eight. But before you jump ahead to those chapters, let's learn more about bullying, beliefs and the difference between a bullyable child and an *Unbullyable* child.

How do children define bullying?

When we put aside the numerous textbook definitions of bullying and ask the experts (the children being bullied), they are very clear about their own experience of bullying. They use their own criteria to decide for themselves if they are being bullied or not, usually by how they *feel* rather than listing the behaviour of the bully. They decide if they are being bullied by how they feel *about* the bullying behaviours directed towards them and what those particular behaviours *mean* to them, rather than the actual behaviours.

Here is a simple definition provided by Ethan, a bullied ten-year-old boy who I asked, *'What is bullying?'*

Bullying is when someone hassles me and they do it a lot – more than just once or twice. They make me feel scared and angry. I don't like it but there is nothing I can do about it.

If we were to keep it simple and consider Ethan's definition, we discover what being bullied means *to him*, and uncover *his* criteria. In those three sentences, he gives us many clues into *what it means to him*. Even if your child chooses not to tell you much about being bullied, the way he describes bullying will give you information about how he experiences it. You can use this information like a road map to help him.

In addition to describing how he feels about being bullied, your child has his own way of describing the behaviours directed towards him by the bully. To help your child, it's important that you speak his 'bullying' language. We explore this more in Chapter Five.

How bullyable is your child?

How is it that some children are seemingly unaffected by bullying, while others are bullied? Some children are regarded as easy targets, while other children seem *Unbullyable*. We know bullying occurs in many different ways and circumstances. Two children can be the target of the same bullying behaviours and one will feel bullied, while the other will feel unaffected. How is this possible?

The simple answer is this: it comes down to the beliefs and meanings of each child. The effectiveness of the bullying behaviour is determined by the meaning your child gives the behaviour. Two children experiencing the same bullying behaviour can have two *very* different interpretations, meanings, belief systems, expectations, understandings, rules etc.

> *The effectiveness of the bullying behaviour is determined by the meaning your child gives the behaviour.*

A bullyable child experiences the bullying behaviour of the bully and believes the bully *makes* him feel scared, intimidated, angry and so on, and feels these feelings. If your child believes someone can *make* him feel powerless, annoyed, intimidated, angry etc., there is a high chance he will experience bullying. The system will work as the bully hopes and anticipates. Your child can't control the bully's behaviour, but he can control how he responds to the bully's behaviour. Your child can learn to think in a different way so he interrupts the pattern. It may seem an impossibility to you right now, but I know this is possible as I have seen hundreds of children learn to choose how they respond to the bully's behaviour. It may not happen overnight, but it is possible. If you are having doubts, hang in there and keep reading.

A bullyable child:
- believes he can be bullied
- believes other people *make* him feel a certain way
- believes other people have power over him
- is inflexible with the meanings he gives to bullying behaviour
- is in an unresourceful state and has no choice of the state he is in when someone tries to bully him
- wants other people to *give* him self-esteem

An *Unbullyable* child
- believes he can choose to be unaffected by other people's attempts to bully him

- believes he chooses what he thinks, feels, says and does
- is flexible in his thinking; can give behaviours several different meanings
- chooses a resourceful state when someone tries to bully him
- esteems himself unconditionally

What clues may indicate your child is being bullied?

While this book has been written for parents of bullied children, you may be reading it because you *suspect or are worried* your child is being bullied and he hasn't told you. Unless your child or someone who knows the situation comes right out and tells you directly, you might not know your child is being bullied.

Don't panic! Thirty-three per cent of boys and twenty-three per cent of girls experiencing bullying ask *no one* for help, which indicates they are highly skilled at keeping it a secret.[3] Children are very creative in hiding the fact they are being bullied from their parents, teachers, friends and siblings. As much as you would like to think you would know or suspect if your child is being bullied, you might not. This is *not* a reflection upon you as a parent.

There are many reasons why your child might not share with you he is being bullied. Reasons include the belief that the bullying will get worse if he speaks up, that he will get in trouble, and not wanting to worry or stress out his parents. Some children fear their parents will rush to the school and make a scene, while others believe they should be able to handle the bullying on their own.

You know your child better than anyone. Follow your intuition if you suspect something is not right. Unfortunately for some children, bullying has such an impact on them that they are overwhelmed, and find it hard to think logically. While most children will eventually tell an adult, some children wait until the bullying is almost unbearable before they tell someone. Some children wait years. Some never tell. Every bullied child I have coached who initially kept the bullying a secret from their parents has shared, *'I wish I had told someone sooner'*.

Consider the following symptoms and behaviours common to bullied children, which may (but not definitely) indicate your child is being bullied. If you already know your child is being bullied, this information may help to explain your child's past or current behaviour.

Behaviours may include:
1. Not wanting to go to school
2. Withdrawing – not wanting to socialise
3. Increased sickness
4. Increased emotional outbursts at home

1. Not wanting to go to school

This is a common symptom of bullying. Most parents instinctively know if something is NQR (not quite right) with their child, especially if their child normally enjoys school. Children start making excuses to miss school so they can avoid the bully. Some older children will miss a particular class to avoid the bully.

While avoiding the bully may seem like a workable short-term solution, eventually the situation becomes too difficult for the child. Many children want to go to school; they just don't want to come face to face with the bully. It's too hard. Your child can learn how to think about bullying so he can continue to go to school, and even be in the same class as the bully.

Thinking which may hold this behaviour in place:
- It's easier to avoid him/her

- It's too hard at school – too tiring
- I'm sick of it
- I'm not hanging around to see what might happen today
- I just can't handle it any more
- If I'm bullied in the morning, my whole day is ruined
- I need a rest from him/her
- The teachers don't care/don't do anything

2. Withdrawing – not wanting to socialise

Children who are bullied often spend recess and lunchtime trying to hang around the school office, staffroom, or teachers to avoid going into the schoolyard. To be seen alone at recess or lunchtime is difficult for some children, as this can make them more of a target. Having friends is extremely important because bullies tend to pick on 'loners'. Your child can learn basic social skills like walking up and joining in with a group, which is vital to decreasing his likelihood of being bullied.

Thinking which may hold this behaviour in place:
- If I stay out of sight s/he won't hassle me
- It's going to happen today
- I need to keep away from my bully
- No one likes me
- My friends don't stick up for me like they should

3. Increased sickness

Many children describe being on 'full alert' at school. They are vigilant about where the bully is at all times, as well as super conscious of how they are seen by other children. As you can imagine, this creates a lot of tension in the body, and the resulting stress has a negative impact on their health. Some children complain of stomach-aches on school mornings but not on weekends. Many children come home from school totally exhausted, even if they were not bullied on that particular day. Your child can learn to use physical symptoms as useful information, rather than be concerned by it.

Thinking which may hold this behaviour in place:
- I need to avoid the bully at all times
- This is never going to end
- This is going to happen every day
- Maybe I am a loser like s/he says
- There is nothing I can do about it

4. Increased emotional outbursts at home

For some children, keeping it together emotionally at school is important. As one child described: *'I don't want my bully to see that he is getting to me.'*

Some children don't want to show any emotions at school, but will explode in the safety of their own home. According to one teenage girl: *'I bottle it all up at school and come home and pick a fight with my mum so I get it all out.'*

A ten-year-old girl explained: *'I hold the anger in at school because if I let it out at school I will get into trouble. At home I get into less trouble, so I scream at my little brother and my mum. It's better that way.'*

Your child can learn to think about his emotions as useful information, rather than something to be swallowed, bottled up, or controlled. He can learn how to accept his emotions, rather than turn them against himself.

Thinking which may hold this behaviour in place:
- I can't let the bully see s/he is getting to me

- Emotions are bad
- Emotions hurt me on the inside, but I'm not going to show it on the outside
- It's not okay to cry at school/in front of other kids
- I can't control my emotions

Chapter summary

- The experience of being bullied is an interaction, something that happens between your child and another child or children.
- Parents who help their child the most are the ones who take the time to educate themselves, and have firstly explored their own thinking and feelings about bullying.
- Most widely found definitions of bullying focus on the behaviour of the bully and ignore the beliefs of the target.
- Most definitions of bullying have these four components: the intention to cause harm; repeated; by one individual or a group against another individual or group; and a power imbalance.
- Exploring the target's beliefs and meanings, as well as the state he experiences, allows for the target to be empowered, rather than powerless.
- For bullying to be successful for the bully, there needs to be a perceived power imbalance by both the bully and the target.
- Your child can learn how to choose what he thinks, believes and how he feels. Yes. He can. Hang in there.
- What your child believes about himself is crucial in his bullying experience.
- The success or failure of the bullying attempt is ultimately determined by the meaning your child gives it.

- For behaviour to be truly successful from the bully's perspective, your child has to give it a negative meaning.
- A bullying attempt is successful for the bully when the target is in an unresourceful state – for example, a state of powerlessness, fear and hurt.
- Your child can choose to move from an unresourceful state to a more resourceful state – for example, a state of curiosity, un-insult-ability and powerfulness.
- When your child learns to choose the state he is in when the bully attempts to bully him, he is a step closer to becoming *Unbullyable*.
- Children decide for themselves if they are being bullied by how they *feel* rather than listing the behaviours of the bully.
- The effectiveness of the bullying behaviour is determined by the meaning your child gives the behaviour.
- Behaviours that may indicate your child is being bullied include not wanting to go to school, not wanting to socialise, increased sickness and increased emotional outbursts at home.

Moving forward

Your child has the ability to take back his *power* instead of giving it away to the bully. With awareness and support, your child can explore his *meanings and beliefs* so he can think in an *Unbullyable* way. Can you imagine your child learning how to step into a *state* of un-insult-ability, strength and powerfulness when facing a bully?

With your help and guidance, your child can do these things! In the next chapter we explore how *your beliefs* about bullying have an impact on how you help your child.

2

Exploring your beliefs about bullying

In the first chapter I clarified what bullying is and introduced the concept that you can help your child move from bullied to *Unbullyable*. This chapter is different because the focus is on you, the parent. In this chapter we explore *your* inner world of bullying.

The purpose of this chapter is to increase your awareness and understanding of your inner world. We will explore how you think about bullying, your child being bullied, and, if you yourself have been bullied, how your own experiences have an impact on how you help your child. Together we explore:

- What is meant by your 'map of the world'?
- How do you create your beliefs?
- How do you create your beliefs about bullying?
- How can you use your emotions to help your child?
- How can increasing your awareness of your meanings, beliefs and emotions be useful in helping your child?

What is meant by your 'map of the world'?

Throughout this book we explore your 'map of the world' regarding bullying. This metaphor has been around since 1933.[4]

It refers to how you think *about* bullying in your mind, your mindset or your frame of mind.

Your map of the world is made up of your beliefs, rules, understandings, hopes, wishes, memories, expectations, 'shoulds' etc. It is accurate at the time you create it, but like a GPS directing you in your car, your map of the world can become outdated and inaccurate. If you use an old map in a new context, you could get lost, take longer to reach your destination, or not reach your destination at all. Unless you constantly check your map of the world is accurate, and update it when necessary, you could spend a lot of time wondering if you should *'Perform a U-turn when possible!'*

How do you create your beliefs?

When you were born your brain was still developing and you had not been conditioned to think or believe anything. As you grew and your brain developed, you had experiences, were exposed to events and incidents, and you began to learn about the world around you. As a young child you also began to form your identity. As you grew older you discovered your personal powers and more complex concepts such as love and time. You began to create your map of the world from what you learnt around you. Your child is now doing exactly the same thing, and you are having an impact on how your child's map of the world is shaped. (Kind of scary!)

You gain an understanding of the world and form your beliefs from your personal experiences, the relationships you have with your parents, siblings, extended family, friends, neighbours, teachers, fellow students, and your interactions with the local community, society, religion and so on. You learn the meaning of external events by noticing the shared meanings within your

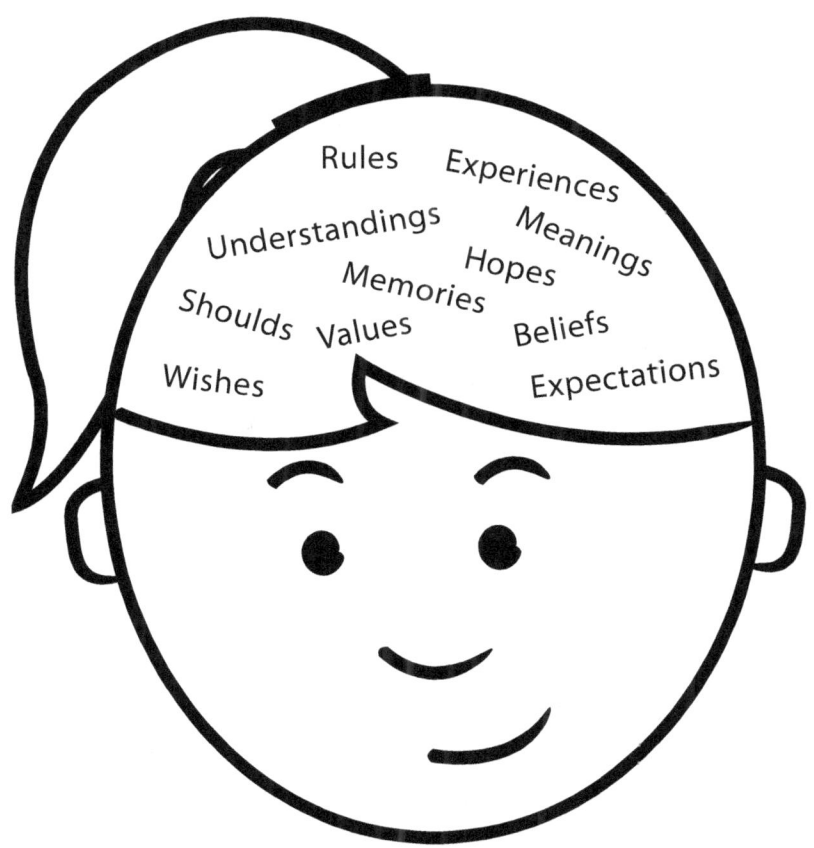

family, culture, society or religion. As a child, you made sense of the world by asking questions, considering what others told you and receiving feedback. As you grew older you started making up your own mind, questioning whether what others told you was true and you began to create your *own meanings*. As an adult, you may have already realised you have the ability to question *even your strongest beliefs*. You may often question the usefulness and value of your beliefs. Some people don't do this, simply because they don't know they can. We may refer to them as *'stuck in their ways'*. This doesn't mean their way of thinking is set in concrete. They can learn to become more flexible in their thinking if they choose to.

How do you create your beliefs about bullying?

As an adult, you have already experienced many years of conditioning about bullying. It is highly likely you already have strong beliefs, rules, understandings, hopes, wishes, memories, expectations, shoulds and so on making up your map of the world about bullying. You also have beliefs about *your children being bullied*. Maybe your beliefs include *'No one will ever, EVER, bully my child'* or *'I know my child is very assertive and confident, and not likely to be bullied'*.

The great thing is you can quality-check the resourcefulness of your thinking regarding bullying. You can step back from your beliefs and ask yourself if they are empowering or not. You can decide if you would like to update your beliefs about bullying and make them more beneficial for you and your child.

Let's start by exploring your current beliefs about bullying. The reason we do this is to see what meanings and beliefs you are bringing to your child's bullying experience.

To explore your beliefs, ask yourself how you were 'conditioned' to think about bullying when you were a child:
- How did you learn what bullying was?
- How did you know to call it bullying and not something else?
- Did your parents teach you not to bully – that bullying is wrong, naughty, unfair or unacceptable? Or did they teach you bullying is how to get what you want?

- Did your school promote certain values on which your understandings of acceptable behaviour were based?
- Did you bully someone and feel guilty, enjoy it or get into trouble?
- Were you bullied or a bully or both as a child?

Taking time to reflect on the above questions allows you to identify your current beliefs about bullying. When you were thinking about these questions, what did you discover about how you thought about bullying as a child? Did you discover any 'rules'?

A clue to discovering your rules is to notice when you use the words *should, must, have to* and *got to*. These words generally indicate a rule. Start by asking yourself where the rule came from. Maybe it was useful when you were a child, but isn't so useful now as an adult. You decide if you want to keep the rule, or change it, or drop it altogether.

You choose how you think about bullying. You don't have to use the same map of the world you used as a child. Consider how you think about bullying now, as a parent:

- Do you have any rules about protecting your child from bullies?
- When you talk about bullying with your child, what language do you use? What is your voice like? Your body language? Your breathing?
- Have you passed any of your ways of thinking about bullying on to your child? In what way, if any, have you influenced her map of the world in relation to bullying?
- Do you have a reaction when hearing the words *bully, bullying* or *bullied*?

As you read the questions, did you notice any changes or sensations in your body? It may be a churning in your stomach, or a tightening of your chest. What do you call that feeling? If you were able to notice where you felt it in your body, fantastic! That is useful feedback, which can be used as information about how you think about bullying.

For some people, even just hearing the word *bullying* causes a reaction in their body. They have associated the word with emotions such as fear, anger or guilt. Their own childhood experiences of bullying strongly impacts how they respond to their child being bullied.

If you were bullied as a child (or an adult, or both) and you believe it would be beneficial to share your experience with your child, you could be of great support to her. To ensure you are not 'lecturing' your child, ask her if you can share your story with her. Let her know you are not telling her what to do; you are sharing some information about how you handled the experience, or what worked for you. Invite your child to just listen and take from your story what she likes. Sharing your own story helps your child to feel she is not alone, and shows her you have an understanding of what it is like to be bullied. It is a way of reassuring your child it does get better – you were bullied, and you got through it.

How can you use your emotions to help your child?

You may find talking about your childhood bullying experience brings out powerful emotions, especially if it was very painful. This is normal and perfectly okay, so long as these emotions are not stopping you from helping and supporting your child *now*. We will explore how you make your emotions work for you in Chapter Nine.

Bec, whose little girl was being bullied, explained her emotions: *'I feel like I am being bullied all over again. I don't want her to go through what I went through. I left school at fifteen because I was being bullied.'*

Michelle, whose teenage daughter was being bullied, was able to see the humour in her reaction to the word *bully*:

My rule was no child of mine would ever be bullied like I was. If I heard my daughter even just use the word bully my ears would prick up and I would feel very defensive and protective. I would immediately start interrogating her by firing endless questions at her. 'Are you being bullied? Who's bullying you? What's her name?' What did she do to you...?' My daughter would be like, 'Whoa Mum, settle, take a chill pill. It's okay. I'm not being bullied.' I guess I was a bit over the top!

Being aware of and noticing if you are bringing your own emotions, expectations, rules, memories and meanings to your child's situation involves stepping back from your current thinking and asking yourself:

- Is this thinking helpful?
- Is this helping my child?
- Is this about me or my child?

We each have our own personal beliefs about bullying and parenting, which influence how we respond to our child being bullied. Some parents consider their child being bullied as a learning experience, an opportunity for their child to explore being assertive, and standing up for herself. This is normally the case when the bullying has been over a brief timeframe and, while their child has been upset, she is coping emotionally.

For other parents, the negative meaning they attach to bullying gets in the way of them helping their child. It's very useful to explore and become aware of what it means to you if your child is being bullied. (If *means* is the wrong word for you, try *equals* instead, or whatever language works for you.)

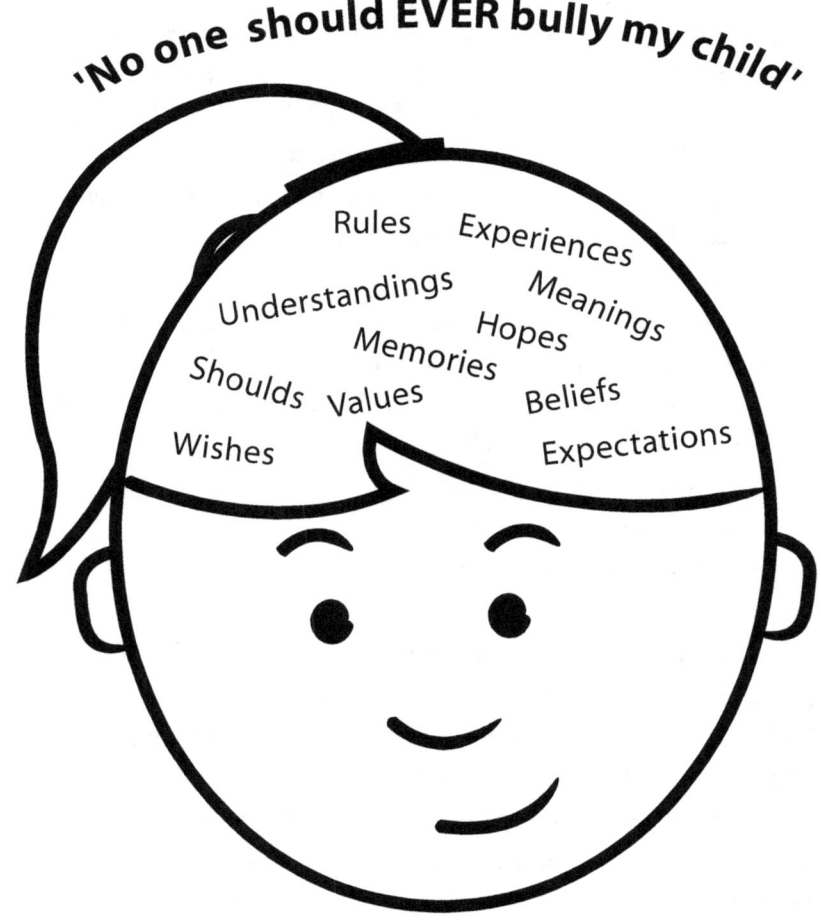

Here are some examples of what parents have shared with me. *'My child being bullied means (equals)'*:
- I have failed as a parent
- I have not protected my child as I should have
- I am to blame for this happening
- I am a hopeless parent
- I have let my child down

If you choose to think about your child being bullied from a negative, or unresourceful view, and think you have failed, not protected, are to blame for having let your child down because you are such a hopeless parent, chances are you are not in the space to help your child. You may even be feeling so disempowered and miserable you are immobilised.

You really don't have to give yourself such a hard time!

You can change the way you think about your child being bullied. Instead of thinking and feeling negatively about what has happened, and probably being of little help to your child, you can choose to think in a more positive way. You created your beliefs and meanings, therefore you can change them to something more resourceful. We explore exactly how to do that in the next chapter.

You can explore your beliefs about bullying to help you identify your helpful, energising and empowering ways of thinking. In addition, as you become more aware of your limiting beliefs, you can question their usefulness. You can ask yourself, *'What if I changed any negative meanings to something that gives me more energy, a clear head and a sense of hope?'* See what it's like to think about your child being bullied in the following ways:
- Even though my child is being bullied, I know I have done my best to protect my child from being harmed

- My child being bullied is not a reflection upon my parenting skills
- I am not to blame for someone trying to bully my child
- I will continue to be the best parent I can be
- I will do everything I can to help my child deal with the bullying she is experiencing
- I choose the meaning I give to my child being bullied
- I choose how I think and feel about my child being bullied, as well as what I do and say

Give yourself permission to 'try on' a different way of thinking about your child being bullied. The term 'trying on' involves giving yourself the flexibility to allow yourself to imagine what it would be like to think in a different way. If you have trouble letting yourself do that, you might like to consider using some of the language in the following points. Give it a try – it might feel strange at first, or you might like to come back to it at a later time:

- Let's say this is true for me, *'that my child being bullied is not a reflection upon my parenting skills'*
- What if *'I am not to blame for someone trying to bully my child'* was true for me?
- I'll try on *'I choose how I think and feel about my child being bullied, as well as what I do and say'* for thirty seconds, just to see if it fits. I can always take it off again.
- If I looked through the eyes of me knowing that *'I have done my best to protect my child from being harmed'*, I would see that...

Notice the *meanings* and *beliefs* you have given to the experience of your child being bullied. Are there any you would like to change, and try on a different way of thinking?

How can increasing your awareness of your meanings, beliefs and emotions be useful in helping your child?

A distinction we make in the field of Neuro-Semantics is that we have a mind–body–emotion system.[5] Our thinking, behaviours and feelings about bullying influence each other. How you think about your child being bullied has an affect on how you feel about it, which influences what you do about it and so on. Cindy shared the meanings, beliefs and emotions she experienced when her child was being bullied:

> *I felt responsible. I felt like I had failed my daughter; that I did not give her the confidence and self-worth she needed to survive in this world. I felt guilty that she had to go through it when it could have been avoided. I questioned my parenting skills and wondered where I had gone wrong. I felt anxious and I didn't feel confident about dealing with it.*

In retrospect, Cindy was able to see her way of thinking about her daughter being bullied was unresourceful in that it did not help her to help her daughter. Her feelings of being a failure, her anxiety and guilt had stood in the way of her being able to empower herself and her daughter. If Cindy had known she could explore and change her map of the world and understand her feelings of failure, anxiety and guilt, she may have been in a better position to help to her daughter.

As Cindy reflected:

> *Hindsight is a wonderful thing! Looking back now, I see I was over-thinking it. I was making it all doom and gloom and forgetting about all the wonderful parenting I have given my daughter. I was making it about me.*

Cindy's initial unresourceful reaction was accurate given how she thought about bullying. The fantastic news is that you don't have to keep thinking or feeling this way if you don't want to. You can change your meanings. You have a choice in how you respond. And that choice comes from exploring the meanings and beliefs you have about bullying and parenting. As Dr L. Michael Hall explains, 'every and any emotion is always right. It is right given the map from which it comes.'[6]

Danni's story

Let's consider Danni's story, as an example of how her childhood bullying experiences impact upon how she now thinks about her role as a mother of two small children. Danni was bullied for three years during high school. She describes how her own bullying experience impacts on the way she thinks about bullying, including what it would mean to her if either of her children were bullied:

> *I was so excited about starting high school. I thought it was going to be amazing. That expectation was squashed out of me very quickly when reality hit. I went from a primary school with fifty-six students to a high school with over a thousand students. There were a lot of tough kids and I didn't know anyone. There was a lot of violence – I witnessed kids bashing each other and teachers doing nothing to stop it. Fear set in. I lived in fear. I lost my love of learning.*

> *In year seven it took me a while to make any friends. I would walk around the school on my own. The bullying started in year seven and continued in year eight and nine. I was bullied by boys mainly, and a few girls. I was bullied because I was a 'wog'. I was small and shy and quiet. They would bully me and*

I never said anything to stick up for myself. I was too scared I would be bashed. I hated school. I hated catching the bus. I was really disappointed, but I came to accept that was how it was. I couldn't concentrate very well on my schoolwork because I was constantly worrying about what would or could happen next.

I never told my parents because I was scared it would get worse. Mum would have gone up to the school and made a scene.

One day in year nine I just snapped. I asked myself why I should have to keep living in fear. I was tired of living in fear. I was over it. I'd had enough. I decided I needed to toughen up. One of the bullies said something to me and I turned around and told him to 'fuck off'. He and his mates were shocked. As they kept trying to bully me I kept saying stuff back to them. I didn't care anymore. I'd had nearly three years of constant harassment, and I was facing another three years unless something changed, and that something was me. Eventually the bullying died down and by year ten it had stopped. A lot of the bullies had left school, and I guess we had all matured a bit.

As an adult I don't hate the bullies who gave me such a hard time in school. If I see them around town, I just let it go. I believe you've got to move on.

Now I have two small children of my own and I am very protective of them. I often say to my husband, 'God help the kid who picks on our kids!' If my children were bullied I'd be devastated. Gut wrenched. They shouldn't have to feel worried and scared and cry like I did. I think it's sad there is still bullying going on in our schools after all these years.

Has my bullying experience affected the way I bring up my children? Yes. My husband and I teach our children to never hurt people. We don't say hurtful things. We ask them, 'How would you like it? Put yourself in their shoes.' I have also taught them if they see someone else being nasty to not join in. Just like no one will ever bully my child – no child of mine will be a bully.

Chapter summary

- It is useful to increase your awareness of how you think about bullying, your child being bullied and, if you yourself have been bullied, how your own experiences have an impact on how you help your child.
- Your 'map of the world' regarding bullying refers to how you think *about* bullying in your mind.
- Your map of the world is made up of your beliefs, rules, understandings, hopes, wishes, memories, expectations, shoulds etc.
- You create your beliefs from your personal experiences, your parents, siblings, extended family, friends, neighbours, teachers, fellow students, local community, society, religion, heroes, and so on.
- As an adult, you have already experienced many years of 'conditioning' about bullying.
- You can quality-check the resourcefulness of your thinking regarding bullying.
- If you were bullied as a child, or an adult, or both, and you believe it would be beneficial to share your experience with your child, you could be of great support.

- We each have our own personal beliefs about bullying and parenting, which influence how we respond to our child being bullied.
- If you choose to think about your child being bullied from a negative, or unresourceful view, and think you have failed, not protected, are to blame or have let your child down because you are such a hopeless parent, chances are you are not in the space to help your child.
- You can change the way you think about your child being bullied. Instead of thinking and feeling negatively about what has happened, and probably being of little help to your child, you can choose to think in a more positive way.
- Your thinking, behaviours and feelings about bullying influence each other. How you think about your child being bullied has an affect on how you feel about it, which influences what you do about it and so on.

Moving forward

Maybe as you read this chapter you discovered some limiting beliefs, 'rules' or expectations that hold you back, and you would like to change them. If you would like to create some flexibility in your thinking, and upgrade your map of the world, read on, because the next chapter explains how to change limiting beliefs into empowering ones.

3

Changing your beliefs about bullying

Now you have increased your understanding of your map of the world, including where your beliefs and meanings come from, we are ready to move on to changing them. This chapter is about freeing yourself of any beliefs that are holding you back from helping your child, and trying on some new, more useful beliefs. In the following pages we will look at you choosing to empower yourself by upgrading your map of the world, and choosing useful, helpful beliefs. Exciting isn't it?

I invite you to explore the following questions:
- How do *your* beliefs play a role in helping your child?
- What is the difference between your thoughts and your beliefs?
- How can you change a thought into a belief, and vice versa?
- How do you create a limiting or toxic belief?
- How can you check if your beliefs are resourceful or limiting?
- What is the process for changing a limiting or toxic belief into an empowering belief?

How do *your* beliefs play a role in helping your child?

In this book we are starting with you first. We explore *your* thoughts, *your* understandings, *your* meanings and *your* beliefs. There is a reason for this. Some years back I conducted a six-month training course for teachers called Empowering Students. While the training was beneficial for the teachers in understanding how students can be empowered to handle bullying among other things, I felt something was missing, but I couldn't put my finger on it. Then one afternoon as I spoke with a teacher at length about how she was finding the training, the penny dropped. She was telling me how she had been implementing what she had learnt in the classroom, all the while using language that indicated *she* was not empowered herself. I asked myself, 'How do I expect her to empower her students when she herself appears disempowered?' In the very next training session we moved the focus from empowering the students to empowering the teachers!

So, in this chapter we begin by offering strategies for you to further empower *yourself*. Once you are clear about how *your* beliefs work, how to quality-check them to see if they are useful for you, and how to change them, you can effectively help your child explore and quality-check *his* beliefs about bullying.

What is the difference between your thoughts and your beliefs?

To start with, some of your thoughts are just thoughts; you don't give them much meaning, power or energy. You think them into existence and then they disappear. They have little effect on you because you know they are just thoughts. You can think things that are not true. You don't *feel* anything when you think them. You have the ability to think things and not confirm them, to not make them true for you. You have the choice to *not* turn certain thoughts into beliefs. You can think something, yet not *believe* it.

> *'I can think things I don't believe.'*

How can you change a thought into a belief, and vice versa?

You have the ability to make the decision that a certain thought is true for you. You can say *'Yes!'* to it. You can take the simple thought and add a robust, *'Yes, it is definitely true!'* to it.

As you confirm the thought as true for you, you send messages throughout your body via your central nervous system and you *feel* the thought as true for you. You embody that thought as a belief. To you it feels right. You may even say, *'I feel strongly about it.'*

Your confirmed thoughts become your beliefs and make up your belief systems. Your beliefs are embodied into your neurology.

How do you create a limiting or toxic belief?

Beware, since you can make *any* thought true for you, you can create beliefs that are poisonous, toxic or limiting to you achieving what you want to achieve. These kinds of beliefs hold you back from reaching your true potential, or even make you sick!

Since you decide what is true for you, you can choose to confirm thoughts that are unresourceful, limiting, and toxic. As Robert Dilts makes clear, a belief does not have to be true to be believed[7]. Wow! I was genuinely shocked when I first read that. A belief does not have to be true for me to believe it. Hmm.

In other words, you can have many negative thoughts about yourself – for example, *'I am stupid'*, *'I am a failure'*, *'I am a bad parent'*, *'I don't deserve to be happy'* and so on, and make those thoughts true for you. Even if there is no evidence to support these thoughts, you will see evidence. You can believe these types of thoughts if you choose to.

Let's consider an example of a toxic thought. If you choose to think, *'I am not good enough'*, and confirm it, make it true for you, and embody it so it sends messages through your nervous system to make it real, then you will believe it. It will seem real to you. You then feel the experience of not being good enough, which affects your behaviour, and you walk around thinking, feeling, acting, knowing and believing you are not good enough. You might even identify with it, *'I am a person who is not good enough'*.

After seeking out and finding evidence to support your belief, you make it permanent: *'I will never be good enough.'* And you can do that for the next forty, sixty, eighty years if you choose to, never questioning the belief. You even confirm it again and again: *'But I feel like I'm not good enough, so it must be true. It's just the way I am.'* Or never question it: *'Good enough for what? Good enough in what way? Good enough according to what criteria? When will I know when I am good enough? When will I ever be good enough?'*

Empowering yourself involves becoming aware of any beliefs that you experience as disempowering. Once you become aware of these limiting beliefs, you can question their effectiveness and change them if you choose to.

So, how do you find your beliefs that are holding you back?

How can you check if your beliefs are resourceful or limiting?

Imagine you could press the pause button on your thinking right now and take a moment to consider all the thoughts you have had today. It's estimated humans have on average seventy thousand thoughts each day. And what makes humans different from other animals is that we have the ability to reflect upon our thoughts. We can think about our thinking.

If you were to step back and think about your thoughts today, what *kind* of thoughts were they? Were they positive, negative or neutral? Were they about the past, present or future? Were they useful or toxic? Were they true or fictional? Can you identify any themes or notice any patterns in your thoughts? Checking the quality of your thoughts begins by firstly being aware of them, and secondly by questioning their usefulness.

One of the great things about your beliefs is they are yours to change any time you choose. At some stage in your life your thoughts were useful; you confirmed them as true for you. They made sense at the time. In your map of the world you found evidence to support your belief. Maybe as a teenager you believed, *'I've fallen out with my three closest friends in the past two years. I'm just not good at staying friends with people. I'm not good at being a friend.'* Now as you look back at that belief as someone older and wiser, you can quality-check it: *'Well, it seemed true as a teenager, but now as an adult, I see this belief is holding me back from connecting with new people.'*

Since you create your beliefs, you can choose to change them, alter them, delete them, replace them, strengthen them, add to them, and so on. The key is to firstly become aware of any of your beliefs that are holding you back from being your

> *Many people don't realise that since they create their beliefs, they can also change them.*

best. Quality-check them by asking yourself questions and, if you need to, create new beliefs that serve you better. You can create beliefs that are more resourceful for you.

I didn't fully realise I could change my beliefs until I was in my early thirties. I assumed my beliefs were set in concrete, and couldn't be changed, including the ones that were not useful. I thought, *'This is just the way I am. This is my personality and I will be thinking and feeling this way for the rest of my life.'* I tried many times to change my behaviour, but the change didn't last. Of course now I know I can quality-check and change my beliefs and meanings. I get to choose who I 'be'. Do you have any limiting beliefs you would like to change? Maybe they are in relation to bullying or parenting? Or perhaps they're about something else?

I've coached women in their fifties and sixties who have burst into tears when they realised they can change their beliefs. Some are genuinely surprised: *'You mean I don't have to keep believing I am unlovable?'* For some women there have been tears of sadness because they have spent so many years believing something about themselves that has stopped them being who they really are, and the best version of themselves. And sometimes there are tears of joy and excitement at the possibilities that lie ahead for them as they move through the world creating new beliefs about themselves.

You have the ability to:
- take charge of your thinking and change your beliefs

- change a thought into a belief by confirming it as true, and saying *'Yes!'* to it
- change a belief back into a thought by dis-confirming it and rejecting the value of believing it
- say 'No!' to the significance and importance of a belief
- take a toxic belief and say *'No!'* to it, until it returns to being just a thought, is de-energised and no longer a belief
- change a toxic belief you have held on to for a long time, even for decades

Let's keep going, and put the theory into practice.

What is the process for changing a limiting or toxic belief into an empowering belief?

Dr L. Michael Hall developed a process for changing a limiting belief, called 'The Belief Change Pattern'. I often use it when coaching children who want to change the belief they can be bullied. The following is a simplified version[8].

Warning! Before you start, be aware this process involves saying things out loud, and moving your body (you will probably want to stand up for this). If you don't want family members wondering if you have finally lost the plot, you might like to find some privacy for yourself so you are able to fully participate, uninhibited!

Do you have a belief you know is limiting you or holding you back – for example, stopping you from helping your child? If you are not sure, consider these questions to get you started:
- What beliefs are holding you back in some way?
- Have you discovered any limiting beliefs you would like to remove from your thinking and feeling?

- Which belief specifically would make the biggest difference to your quality of life if you change it?

Choose a specific belief to explore. As you think about that belief, ask yourself what is it you would like to move away from:
- How is this limiting belief getting in your way?
- How does this limiting belief sabotage you or your effectiveness?
- Have you had enough of this limiting belief? Or would you like to hang on to it for the next twenty, forty or sixty years?

Think about what you would like to move towards:
- What empowering belief would you like to have instead of the limiting one?
- Is the new belief realistic?
- Does the new belief enhance all areas of your life?

Once you are clear about the unresourceful, limiting or toxic belief you are moving away from, leaving behind and saying *'No!'* to, you are ready to move towards and say *'Yes!'* to your new belief. Let's begin.

1. Find your most powerful *'No!'* and step into it
- Think of something every fibre of your body says *'No!'* to in a way that works for you. Use an extreme example, like, *'Would you pour acid into the eyes of your child?'* *'NO WAY!!'*
- Say *'No!'* out loud, and repeat it again and again until you notice the sound of your voice, see a snapshot in your mind, and feel the feeling of saying *'No!'* in your body.

- Use a hand gesture to anchor the feeling in your body. For example, you might push your hand out like a stop sign as you say 'No!', or make a fist. Do whatever feels comfortable and true for you.

2. Say 'No!' to your old limiting belief
- State the old, disempowering belief you want to change – for example, 'I am not good enough'. Take all the power and energy of the 'No!' you used in step one and use the voice, feeling and gesture to say the same 'No!' to this particular limiting belief. Repeat it again and again, until you feel it throughout your entire body.
- Add even more energy to your 'No!' as you think about all the harm, uselessness and wasted opportunities this limiting belief has resulted in for you.
- Keep repeating your powerful 'No!' using your hand gesture, and kick the limiting belief away, shrink it down and suck the life out of it until it's an empty shell of a belief and has no value left in it.
- Use your 'No!' to stubbornly refuse to let the limiting belief back into your thinking by using your voice, tone and gestures to totally dis-confirm that old belief.

3. Find your most powerful 'Yes!', then step into it and turn it up
- Think of something every fibre of your body says 'Yes!' to without any question or doubt – for example, *'Do you love your child?'*
- Notice how it feels in your body when you say 'Yes!' unconditionally. What is the voice of that 'Yes!'? What are

the eyes? The breathing? The posture? What is the overall feeling that goes with your absolute *'Yes!'*?
- Use a hand gesture to anchor the feeling of *'Yes!'* in your body. For example, you might hold your hand to your heart as you say *'Yes!'* Now turn up the feeling of *'Yes!'* until you feel you are about to explode.

4. Say *'Yes!'* to your new empowering belief
- Say out loud the new belief you would like to put into your body. For example, 'I am valuable and worthwhile just for being born.' Take all the feelings of your *'Yes!'* you used in step three and use the same voice, feeling and gestures to say *'Yes!'* as you welcome in your new belief. Try it on. See how it feels. Modify it if you have to until it feels very comfortable. *(Yeah baby, I like the feel of this belief!)*
- Turn the *'Yes!'* up fully as you say *'Yes!'* repeatedly to your new belief. Add even more *'Yes!'* to it as you ask yourself, *'Do I really want this?'* Say *'Yes!'* repeatedly as you think about all the possibilities that await you as you move through the world with this powerful belief. Say *'Yes!'* to the benefit and value in this belief.
- Keep repeating your powerful *'Yes!'* and using your gesture until you believe with every cell in your body that you have fully welcomed in this belief.

5. Say *'Yes!'* to the *'Yes!'* as you think about your future
- Have you definitely decided to own this belief? (*Yes!*)
- Would this improve your quality of life? (*Yes!*)
- Is this belief valuable to you and your future? (*Yes!*)

- As you look forward, can you imagine your life with this belief? Today? Tomorrow? Next week? Next year? In thirty years…? (*Yes!*)

6. Repeat your *'Yes!'*

You can choose to repeat this process five or six times, or however many times it takes, until this new belief feels like a certainty. If you catch yourself in moments of doubt, or feel the old belief raising its head, use your body to say *'Yes!'* to your new belief. Use your gesture, breathing, posture and voice to step back into your *'Yes!'* If done discreetly, you can do this around other people and no one would know!

If the process felt a little strange or weird, let it be that, and give yourself permission to feel strange or weird. You are exploring with thinking and feeling in a new way. You are trying something different and stepping out of your usual way of thinking and feeling. The point of this book is to help you help your child learn to think differently about bullying. Experiencing a belief change yourself will help you achieve that.

This is a great start, and by the end of the book you will have many more strategies to add to this Belief Change process. Congratulations on giving it a go! Here is a story about a coaching client who also gave the Belief Change process a go.

Fran's story

Fran was a lady in her early fifties who was exploring her unresourceful beliefs. She was experiencing bullying in the workplace, yet she found herself unable to speak up about it because her limiting belief about herself was *'I'm no good at confrontation'*. She was genuinely surprised when she realised she could change her beliefs.

> *I just thought this was my personality, who I was. I wished I could speak up for myself, but I just couldn't. I would get very nervous and couldn't think properly. My voice would quiver and I would get sweaty armpits. The idea of me saying something to my boss was just not a possibility in my mind. But I couldn't see the situation changing by itself. Before coaching I had no idea I could change. I thought I had to put up with being bullied and it was my job to manage my stress as best I could.*

Fran described how her thinking was holding her back from going for job promotions, speaking up at meetings, and taking a stand against the bullying co-worker. In coaching, Fran was given information about beliefs and how she creates them and offered a process to change her beliefs. Initially, Fran had her doubts, as she explained:

> *I'm a very loyal person. I've been married for twenty-four years. I've worked in this organisation for nineteen years. I guess I'm loyal to my toxic beliefs too [laughing]. The idea of changing my beliefs terrifies me. Who would I be? How would I function in the world? Without my familiar beliefs I would disappear. I know they are unresourceful, but they are safe, familiar and me. I'm not sure I can change them.*

Fran felt safe enough in the coaching session to 'try on' a new way of thinking and decided to give the Belief Change process a go:

> *I realised something about myself. Sounds strange, but I realised I am more than my beliefs. I can change my beliefs and still be me. I found I didn't have to change every single belief, just the main*

ones that were holding me back. For the first time in a long time I feel like I have choice in who I am as a person.

Fran went on to explore more limiting beliefs and replace them with empowering ones. As her beliefs changed, so did her behaviours. She reported her problematic co-worker to the CEO of her organisation, took on a management position, and eventually left the organisation to work in a much higher paying role in another organisation. Then she left her husband of twenty-four years, and ran off with a much younger man. I'm just kidding! It was true up until the husband part. She tells me she is a lot happier in herself, and still very happily married!

Chapter summary

- Once you are clear about how *your* beliefs work, how to quality-check them, and how to change them, you can effectively help your child explore and quality-check *his* beliefs about bullying.
- Your thoughts are just thoughts – you don't give them much meaning, power or energy.
- You can think something yet not *believe* it.
- You have the ability to make the decision that a certain thought is true for you.
- As you confirm a thought as true for you, you send messages throughout your body via your central nervous system and you *feel* the thought as true for you.
- The thoughts you have decided and confirmed as true for you become your beliefs.
- You can create beliefs that are poisonous, toxic or limiting to you achieving what you want to achieve.

- Empowering yourself involves becoming aware of any beliefs you have decided are true for you that are disempowering you, stopping you from being your best, or limiting you.
- Checking the quality of your thoughts begins by firstly being aware of them, and then secondly, questioning their usefulness.
- Since you create your beliefs, you can choose to change them, alter them, delete them, replace them, strengthen them or add to them.
- Many people don't realise that since they create their own beliefs, they can also change them.

Moving forward

Take some time to explore any limiting beliefs you have, especially in regard to bullying, and how you can help your child. I encourage you to re-read the previous chapters and give yourself the time and space you need to absorb and process the information. When you are ready, I invite you to switch the focus from *your* inner world to the inner world of your child.

In the next chapter we explore how your child thinks about bullying. We look at what children believe and the meanings they give to their bullying experiences.

4

Your child's beliefs about bullying

It is time to focus on how your child thinks and what she believes about bullying, and being a target of bullying. If you are ready, I invite and encourage you to switch focus from *your* inner world to the inner world of your child.

Now we have explored how you create your beliefs, and how you can change them, we are ready to explore your child's beliefs about bullying, and assist her to change her beliefs if *she* wants to. In this chapter we explore:

- What do many bullied children believe about bullying?
- How do your beliefs influence your child's beliefs?
- How do *you* describe bullying in front of your child?
- Why should *your* child change her beliefs?
- How do beliefs hold behaviour in place?

What do many bullied children believe about bullying?

Just as you create your map of the world about bullying, so does your child. Exploring your child's beliefs is not about judging them as right or wrong. The important question is: are your child's beliefs helping her to be *Unbullyable*? Being aware of your child's map of the world is crucial if your goal is to empower her to change her unresourceful beliefs about bullying to resourceful beliefs. Consider these examples of responses from bullied children when asked the question, 'What do you believe about bullying?'

- Bullying is wrong! It is bad! I hate bullies. They are the enemy. I wish they would die or get put in jail
- Mum says I am sensitive and that's why I am being bullied. She says to get used to it because she was the same and she got bullied when she was at school
- I am so sick of being bullied, it's been going on for three years and I have another three years of bullying to go (until I finish school)
- I am going to get picked on because I am quiet and can't stick up for myself
- No one should ever bully anyone. Ever

The children were also asked a slightly different question: 'What do you believe about *you* being bullied?' These were some of their responses:

- I will always be bullied
- I can be bullied
- There is something wrong with me. I must be a retard
- I am weak
- I'm a freak. Maybe what they say about me is true

Can you see how these types of beliefs could potentially result in your child being bullyable? An *Unbullyable* child generally does not have these types of beliefs.

Telling a child to change her behaviour without firstly changing her beliefs is not effective in moving her towards becoming

Unbullyable. Yet this is what many well-intentioned parents, teachers and counsellors do. In contrast, helping your child understand she can choose to change her beliefs is very powerful. Letting your child know she has a choice in what she believes, how she sees herself and the meaning she gives to the behaviour of the bully will enable her to have a different bullying experience.

How do your beliefs influence your child's beliefs?

Do you ever hear yourself saying something to your child and suddenly think, *'Oh my gosh! I sound like my mother! I'm turning into my mother!'* Sometimes my mother's words roll off my tongue as I talk to my own children – especially if I'm feeling frustrated with them. Even though my mother died when I was in my early teens, I still catch myself saying her words. This is an example of how her map of the world has had an influence on my map of the world. A coaching client, Michelle, described how she became aware she had taken on her mother's map of the world in regard to the bullying she was experiencing.

Michelle's story

Michelle is sixteen years old. Before coaching she described herself as an easy target and stated she had been bullied all her life. Michelle wanted to know why she seemed to attract bullies. During our fourth coaching session, Michelle had a breakthrough. When asked a question about her feelings of sadness, the following line rolled effortlessly from her mouth, as if she'd said it a million times before: *'Things have to get worse before they get better'*.

I repeated her words back to her so she could hear herself. Then I asked her, *'Is that what you believe, that things have to get worse before they get better? In what way is this statement relevant to you being bullied?'*

Michelle's eyes filled with tears, and then she smiled:

I don't know why I said that. I think my mum says it. I must believe that things have to get worse before they get better, but I've never really thought about why I believe that it is true…Maybe I've been trying to make the bullying worse and waiting and expecting and hoping that things will get better. Only it's not getting better. It's just getting worse. I see now what I'm doing. I see I could go on waiting forever *for things to get better. Wow. That's awesome!*

In the next coaching session Michelle decided she didn't believe the 'bullying had to get worse before it got better'. She gave herself permission to 'try on' the idea of the bullying having less of an impact on her *now*, rather than waiting for an unspecified amount of time to pass. This was part of her journey towards becoming *Unbullyable*.

How do *you* describe bullying in front of your child?

What you believe about your child being bullied and how you express it in front of her is very influential on how she creates her beliefs about bullying. Be aware of your words and choose them carefully when speaking about bullying with your child. For example, referring to the child doing the bullying as 'your' bully implies the bully belongs to your child. Your child does not own the bully, or the bully's behaviour. Labeling your child as an easy target or one who is likely to be bullied, especially in front of her, can be detrimental to your child's self-image. If your child is walking around believing she will be bullied, she might as well hold up a huge sign saying 'PLEASE COME AND BULLY ME'.

I have heard parents speaking about their children – and sometimes in front of them – saying things like:
- You've got to admit, he's a bit different. You can tell he's going to be picked on. I'm really worried the other kids are going to eat him alive when he starts high school next year
- She's so sensitive; too sensitive. She takes everything anyone says about her personally
- I've thought about changing him to a different school but I think he'll just be picked on there too. There are bullies in every school and he is such an easy target
- He's really shy. Always has been. There's nothing he can do about it. It's genetic. He's just like his father
- I was bullied so I'm not surprised my daughter is too. It's our personality type, our nature, the way we are. We find confrontation hard

Can you imagine what children think when they hear their parents make these kinds of statements? Their thoughts would be along these lines:
- I should be worried about starting high school because I'm going to be bullied
- I'm sensitive. I'm too sensitive. There's something wrong with me
- Even if I change schools I will be bullied. I will be bullied at every school
- I'm shy. I can't change
- My mum was bullied so I will be too. Confrontation is hard and I better avoid it

Why should *your* child change her beliefs?

I can imagine some of you are thinking, 'Hang on a minute, why should *my* child change her beliefs? She's not the one doing the bullying!' Some parents are defensive when I offer a different way of thinking and speaking about bullying. They believe the *bully* should be the one who should change. And yes, I agree with them. It would be wonderful if the child doing the bullying changed his/her thinking and behaviour so s/he doesn't feel the need to bully, but that is something out of our control.

When I've presented this opinion at conferences I have had people respond by accusing me of blaming the victim. To be clear, I am not blaming your child in any way for the bullying behaviour another child might direct towards her. A bully is always responsible for his/her behaviour. No one *makes* someone bully another person. What I'm talking about here is whether your child has any limiting beliefs that are making her an easy target for bullying.

Here are some possible *beliefs* to listen out for when you're talking with your child about bullying:

- I will *always* be bullied
- There is *nothing* I can do about it
- I will *never* have *any* friends
- People *make* me feel sad, angry, scared, worried, upset
- I can't help how I feel
- I can't control my feelings
- I *have* to ignore them
- I can be bullied
- I am an easy target
- If I was a bully I would pick on me
- *No one* likes me, *everyone* picks on me
- People *always* pick on me

Did you notice the limiting beliefs in these statements? Those beliefs set children up to be affected by bullying.

The great news is that all these beliefs can be changed. They don't have to be permanently etched into children's minds. Children can learn to become aware of, explore, quality-check and change their beliefs if they choose to. Most cultures and societies don't promote this fact. Unfortunately, our schools don't teach our children 'Introduction to Belief Creation'. Until that happens, we can lead by example, and let our children know they have choice in what they believe about themselves.

How do beliefs hold behaviour in place?

If your child doesn't know she has choice in what she believes, it can be more difficult for her to change her behaviour. For example, telling your child to 'stand up for herself' when she believes 'there's nothing I can do about being bullied' simply won't work. Until your child chooses to change her unresourceful beliefs regarding bullying, any behavioural strategies that focus solely on behaviour change will be neither successful nor sustainable. In other words, change is needed in beliefs *and* behaviours.

Joel's story

Consider the story of Joel, a seven-year-old boy who, much to the horror of his parents and teacher, wanted to be friends with a bully. They repeatedly told him to keep away from the child bullying him, yet Joel would play with him day after day, and even seek him out.

After two coaching sessions with Joel, I still didn't have an understanding of how his map of the world was structured in relation to the bully. I wondered what belief was holding this behaviour in place. Then I casually asked him a simple question: *'How do you choose your friends?'*

Joel stared at me and answered, *'I don't choose them. You've got to be friends with everybody.'*

Bingo! There it was – the belief that was holding Joel's behaviour in place. By listening to him in a non-judgemental way, I discovered Joel had a belief around *friendship* that held his behaviour in place. His language gave me a clue to there being a rule: *'You've got to be* friends with everybody'.

As we explored Joel's rules, he shared with me:

- *You have to/should be friends with everybody*
- *You can't not be friends with somebody*
- *You can't stop being friends with somebody*

Aha! Now we were getting somewhere!

Yet there was something else missing. Joel was a cooperative boy so why would he go against his parents' and teacher's instructions to keep away from the bully? When I asked him about following rules, and being 'good', he stated that it was very important for him to follow rules. But it didn't make sense that Joel would break his parents' and teacher's rule not to play with the bully.

I asked him, *'You know how you told me "You've got to be friends with everybody" – whose rule is that?'*

'That's God's rule.'

Of course! Joel came from a very religious family. I could see how his behaviour of playing with the bully made sense to him according to his map of the world. God's rule, that he *'should be friends with everybody'*, kept him interacting with the bully. In Joel's mind, God's rule was 'bigger' than his parents' and his teacher's instruction to keep away from the bully. There was no way Joel was going to break *'God's rule'*!

Joel explained: *'You have to be friends with everybody because God says so...and if you break God's rule you don't go to heaven to be with all your family when you die.'*

Joel had very strong motivation to try to stay friends with the bully! Once he was able to explore and quality-check his rule, he made the finer distinction between being *friendly* towards people and being friends with them. Joel gave himself permission to be friendly towards, but not friends, with the bully. (He did want to check this out with his parents to make sure he wasn't breaking God's rule.)

Much to the relief of his parents, Joel no longer needed to hang around with the bully. After only a few short weeks Joel had made a new friend and the bully had started bullying another child. Joel's story demonstrates how changing a seemingly unrelated belief, even slightly, can result in a significant change in behaviour.

Chapter summary

- You create your map of the world about bullying, as does your child.
- Being aware of your child's map of the world is crucial if your goal is to empower her to change her unresourceful beliefs about bullying to resourceful beliefs.
- *Telling* a child to change her behaviour without firstly changing her beliefs is not effective in her moving towards becoming *Unbullyable.*
- Letting your child know she has choices in what she believes, how she sees herself and the meaning she gives to the behaviour of the bully will enable her to have a different bullying experience.

- Just as your parents' beliefs influenced your map of the world when you were growing up, you are influencing your child's beliefs about bullying.
- Be aware and choose your words carefully when speaking about bullying with your child.
- You have a *huge* impact on the way your child thinks. You can help her change her unresourceful beliefs to resourceful ones.
- A bully is always responsible for his/her behaviour. No one *makes* someone bully another person.
- Children can learn to become aware of, explore, quality-check and change their beliefs if they choose to.
- If your child doesn't know she has choice in what she believes, her beliefs hold her behaviour in place.
- Until your child has decided to change her unresourceful beliefs in regard to bullying, behavioural strategies for dealing with bullying that focus only on behaviour change will be neither successful nor sustainable.
- Changing a seemingly unrelated belief, even slightly, can result in a significant change in behaviour.

Moving forward

So far we have pulled apart many different aspects of the bullying experience. In the next chapter we move to practical skills and explore how you *communicate* with your child about bullying. For some parents this is easy, while others find it difficult to know how to raise the topic in the first instance, or how to respond if their child simply will not discuss the topic. The next chapter includes step-by-step processes so you can have a useful, positive conversation with your child.

5

Conversations about bullying

Okay, I can imagine some of you thinking, '*Oh please! A chapter on how to more effectively communicate with my child???*' I'm a mother of three children, one of whom is a teenager. I acknowledge that when I'm coaching other people's children they tell me things they wouldn't tell their parents because *I'm not their parent.* I'm at a distance from the everyday interactions. I'm not emotionally involved, so I see things from more of an objective viewpoint. I'm presenting this information to make conversations with your children easier for you. Keep in your mind that you are doing your best knowing that you *are* emotionally involved and your ability to communicate *is clouded* by the love, frustration, hopes and dreams you have for your precious child. So with that framework in mind – let's get started!

Together we will explore:
- How do children want their parents to respond?
- What are ten strategies for communicating with your child?

The purpose of this chapter is to offer you strategies, including step-by-step processes so you can have a useful, positive conversation with your child about bullying. So far we have been exploring how you and your child think about bullying, now we will explore how you *communicate* with your child about bullying.

While some parents find communicating easy, others find it difficult. For example, some parents struggle to know how to raise the topic in the first instance, others try many times and are met with a brick wall as their child totally shuts down, or lashes out at them. Consider Mae's experience:

> *My son told me he is being bullied but he won't let me help him. Every time I try to talk to him he gets angry and says he doesn't want to talk about it. It's frustrating for me. I just want to help him, but I'm not sure where to start.*

If you find communicating about bullying with your child easy, fantastic! Take the information in this chapter and apply it to communicating with anyone – your spouse, boss, staff, child's teacher or school principal. Use the information to improve how you communicate with *anyone.*

Imagine sharing this information with your child to improve his communication skills. You can! I use these strategies with children as young as seven years old. Why would you do this? Children with good communication skills are more likely to have friends – and bullies often target children who lack friends.

How do children want their parents to respond?

Since 2007 I have been listening to children speak about their bullying experience and I ask them, 'What is the best way for your parents to help?' Time and time again they answer, *'To listen and believe me.'* What most children want is for their parents to listen to them, believe them, and 'be' with them.

You can be of great support to your children by listening, remaining silent, and holding a safe space for them. Give them your time, even if it's for only a few moments, without spilling your emotional response all over them. If you truly listen, they will often tell you directly how to help. As Grace, aged seventeen, simply put it:

> *When I first told my parents about the bullying I wanted them to say something like, 'Oh my god, I didn't realise', and then to just listen to me without saying anything. Not telling. Not correcting. Not saying their opinion. Not telling me I need to change. Not telling me I need more resilience.*

Annie, aged sixteen, shared how her mum immediately tried to fix things:

> *One day after school I finally told my mum about the bullying and she stressed about it all night. Even though I begged her not to, she went straight to the school the next morning. She wanted to fix it, but she didn't ask me what I wanted, or what I thought would help. I wanted her to go to the school, but not straight away. The very next afternoon I had to meet with the principal and tell her what was going on, and I wasn't ready. I would have rather done that later, after I felt a bit stronger. I wasn't angry at Mum or anything, I know she loves me and was trying to help me – I'm lucky. But I wished she had slowed down a bit.*

What are ten strategies for communicating with your child?

One of the aspects of Neuro-Linguistic Programming (NLP) I have found very useful when coaching is the NLP communication model.[9] I have summarised the information in that model and offer it to you as a set of ten strategies to use when communicating with your child. You may *assume* you are doing a great job, or a terrible job, but unless you actually ask your child how he experiences the conversation, you don't really know. If the purpose of your communication is to support and encourage your child, how do you know you are achieving your goal unless you ask him?

Your method of communication may be face-to-face interaction, over the phone, text message, via Facebook or a mixture of all these. Whatever method you use, let's explore each of these ten strategies:

1. Create your best state for communicating
2. Get yourself out of the way
3. Establish rapport with your child by matching him
4. Pre-frame the conversation
5. Listen, *truly* listen
6. Remain non-judgemental
7. Use questions rather than telling
8. Respond when your child says, '*I don't know*'
9. Give feedback to your child
10. Use sensory-based feedback

1. How can you create your best state for communicating with your child?

The 'state' you are in refers to the combination of your mental, physical and emotional states. We are always in a state. As you read this book, notice what state you are in. Are you in a curious, relaxed and open-minded state?

When we communicate with someone, we communicate from our state to the other person's state. If you want to have a calm, rational conversation with your child and you are feeling angry, frustrated or overwhelmed, your plan will probably fail. Your child might end up in a defensive state, and that would be the end of the conversation! (In Chapter Eight I invite you to be aware of your state, create your ideal state and then step into your best state for communicating with your child.)

2. How can you get yourself out of the way to fully support your child?

To have a supportive conversation with your child it's essential you get yourself out of the way. To truly listen, enter into the world of your child to understand him. Imagine yourself as him. Leave your judgments at the front door and listen for *your child's* meanings, understandings and map of the world. As your child speaks with you about his bullying experience, create a picture in your mind of how it is for him. You might be surprised by what you learn when you don't assume your child's meanings are the same as yours. Ask yourself:

- What meanings, beliefs, experiences, emotions and rules am I bringing to this conversation?
- Do I assume my child shares my beliefs?
- Do I assume my child shares my meanings without actually checking if he does?

Getting yourself out of the way involves having the flexibility to enter into your child's experience of the world, even if you don't necessarily agree with it. Entering into your child's reality does *not* mean you have to agree with how he thinks about bullying. Maintain *your* reality, and your beliefs while understanding how your child perceives his experience. By doing this you are developing the flexibility to temporarily assume your child's words are accurate, correct and true for him. While you listen, resist the temptation to disagree, correct, disregard, ignore, judge or tell him to stop over-reacting.

Step-by-step: getting yourself out of the way
1. Focus your attention on your child
2. Listen without judgement as you enter into the world of your child. Imagine what it is like for him
3. Leave your judgements at the front door and listen for *your child's* meanings, understandings and map of the world
4. Create a picture in your mind of your child's map of the world
5. Temporarily assume your child's words are accurate, correct and true for him

3. How can you establish rapport with your child?
For face-to-face communication with your child, it's best to be in rapport with him. Use your body language to create rapport. Your body language sends the message, *'I'm here with you in this, we are together'*, without you having to say anything. Being in rapport helps your child feel comfortable with your presence, and the conversation. Building rapport with your child enables you to connect with him and enter his world. This is useful if you want to understand your child's bullying experience.

It's common for children to say, *'Finally someone gets me'*, when they are in rapport with someone who is truly listening. You can experience this kind of rapport with your child. It may sound strange to think about actively getting in rapport with your own child, but it makes a big difference. If you are face to face, match your child's posture, and then match his voice and use his exact words. If you're communicating online, match the style of communication. For example, when texting, or messaging on Facebook, use his terminology. He will probably text *thx* and *think ur gr8 lol!*

An effective strategy you can use to build rapport with your child is to 'match' him. Matching is like copying your child, but not copying him exactly, which might be perceived as mimicking. It's a way of being familiar to him, so he will feel comfortable and safe. For example, if your child is seated at the table and you are standing at the table, you are out of rapport and the conversation might feel a bit awkward for him. You are not 'with' him, like you would be if you were sitting next to him at the table. If he has his arms crossed and you're using yours to make huge gestures in the air, you are not in rapport. If your child's voice is barely audible and you are speaking very loudly, almost shouting, you are not in rapport.

Even *before* you say anything, build rapport with your child non-verbally by matching his:
- head tilt
- facial expressions (smiles, frowns, blinks, swallows)
- shoulder angle
- body lean
- posture
- breathing depth and speed
- arms
- legs
- feet
- gestures

You can also match him verbally, by matching his:
- exact words
- laughter
- voice speed
- voice volume
- voice tone
- breathing

Don't wait until an awkward moment with your child and then suddenly try to be in rapport with him. As soon as you put this book down, start practicing getting into rapport with your child (or spouse, child's teacher, boss, friend, bank manager). To begin with you may feel like people think you're copying them, *but they will have no idea!* It's fun once you start doing it, especially at a party where you can practice matching many different people during a short time-frame. Experiment and have fun with it!

Step-by-step: establishing rapport with your child
1. Become aware of your child's posture
2. Notice your own posture
3. Change your posture so you are similar to your child's, but not exactly
4. Become aware of your child's voice, words, tone, silences, breathing etc.
5. Become aware of your own voice, words, tone, silences, breathing etc.
6. Change your voice, etc. so you are similar to your child's, but not exactly

4. How can you pre-frame the conversation?

Another strategy you can use is to 'pre-frame' the conversation. Pre-framing, or setting the scene before you begin the conversation, is a useful method of preparing your child to receive feedback. If your child is unusually sensitive, tearful or you feel you have to walk on eggshells around him and carefully choose every word, then pre-framing is for you! You might say something like, *'I'm going to share something I've noticed about you. It's not a criticism, or a judgement, it's just an observation.'* Or, *'I want you to know I'm here to support you, and I care about you. I'm trying my best to help you.'* Another common pre-frame you might want to explore with your older child is, *'Feedback is information you can choose to use if you want to'*.

5. How can you listen, *truly* listen?

Have you ever been engaged in a conversation to the point where you've lost track of time? Maybe you've been so present to the person you are speaking with that you've noticed a change in their posture, eye cues, even in their breathing. If so, then you have been truly listening. It is likely that if your child feels listened to, he will feel safe, cared for, supported, acknowledged, respected and understood. Steven Covey, author of *Seven Habits of Highly Effective People*, stated that 'seeking first to understand' was one of those seven habits. Seek first to understand your child.

You can be of great support to your child by listening, *truly* listening. Some children describe their parents as responding angrily, jumping to conclusions, telling them what to do, going directly to the school and trying to fix it. The parents' intention is to protect their child, but sometimes this knee-jerk reaction makes things worse for the child who is being bullied. This is not what the child wants in the first instance.

> *Give yourself permission to not have all the answers.*

To improve your ability to listen, take the pressure off yourself. You don't *have* to know what to say! The first thing you can do is to give yourself permission to *not* have all the answers. It's okay not to know what to say or do. No one is expecting you to be able to stop the bullying within minutes of your child telling you about it. It's normal to experience emotions such as anger, worry, sadness or frustration. It's human to want to protect your child. Be kind to yourself, give yourself a break, and when you are ready, ask yourself the following questions:

1. If I am being the best I can be for my child, what is the best, most supportive way to respond?
2. If I am supporting my child as best I can, what is the most resourceful way for me to act, feel, think or say?

Children are more clever and resourceful than we sometimes give them credit for. If they detect even the *slightest hint* of judgemental or condescending language, you can say goodbye as they slam the door of communication firmly shut. We try to support our children, but we don't always get it right. In 2012 I asked teenagers aged between twelve to sixteen years what parents say about bullying and bullies that doesn't help. In fact, what 'advice' *really annoys* them:

- You just need to get some more self-esteem/self-confidence/resilience

- Ignore them and they will go away
- Sticks and stones...(Oh please, not that one!)
- Why don't you close your Facebook account?
- What are you doing to cause this?
- You should keep away from the bullies
- You need to stand up for yourself...deal with it
- Toughen up princess...
- That's nothing. When I was at school I...

Children want us to say less and listen more. To find out if you are a *good* listener, you could ask for feedback from your family and friends (so long as you're prepared to listen to their answers!). Alternatively, Dr L. Michael Hall and Michelle Duval developed benchmarks to measure the presence or absence of listening skills when certifying coaches.[10] With their permission I have tweaked their work and applied it to the context of having a conversation with your child about bullying.

Use these benchmarks as a guide:
- Do you allow time for your child to speak? Are you quiet most of the time? Are you talking less than about thirty per cent of the time?
- Do you turn your body towards your child when you are listening to him?
- Do you look your child in the eyes when you are listening to him?
- Do you nod your head and say, *'Yep, okay'*, or something similar to indicate to your child you are listening to him?
- Do you ask questions about what your child has shared with you rather than changing the subject?

- Are you using your child's specific words or phrases rather than rewording them into your own language?
- Do you allow time for silences, so you are with your child and hold the space for him?

You may be doing all these things already, and naturally. It doesn't hurt to check in with yourself the next time you are listening to your child.

6. How is it possible to remain non-judgemental?

Some children give themselves a hard time about being bullied: they constantly self-judge, self-evaluate and self-doubt. As a parent, you are in the perfect situation to support your child if you find he is beating himself up about being bullied. One teenage girl shared with me when she was being bullied she wanted love, support and reassurance from her family.

If you are planning a conversation with your child, before you begin, ask yourself these questions to clarify your purpose or intention in having the conversation:

- Is the purpose of the conversation to reflect back to my child so he sees himself and then decides if *he* wants to change?
- Is the purpose of the conversation to let my child know I understand him, I hear him, and I am here for him?
- Is the conversation about me feeling better, trying to help my child, or both?

Remaining non-judgemental allows you to fully hear your child.

- Is the purpose of the conversation to provide my child with the support of having someone who listens and believes him? Could I be that person for my child? If not me, then who?

For example, what happens if you remain curious about how your child experiences bullying? Imagine being respectful about what being bullied means to him, and grateful he is sharing with you. It's easier to remain non-judgemental when you are curious, respectful and grateful. Coming from a place where you 'know nothing' is a big help too. This means you are listening as a learner, not as the expert.

Step-by-step: remaining non-judgemental
1. Be in your best state for listening – for example, the state of love, respect, curiosity, support and reassurance for your child
2. Before you begin, ask yourself about your purpose or intention of the conversation
3. Be curious about how your child experiences bullying
4. Come from a place where you 'know nothing'
5. Take on the role of the learner rather than the expert
6. Be open and respectful of your child's map of the world

7. Why use questions rather than tell?
From their perspective, some children can feel they are told what to do by adults all day, and they are tired of it! When you have a different style of conversation, one in which you ask rather than tell, most children respond positively. This is because the dynamics are changed from *'I'm the expert, you need me to tell*

you what to do' to *'you have many resources within you'*. It's about trusting that, with your guidance, your child will come up with his own answers.

The aim of your questions is to increase your child's self-awareness, or help him to clarify his thoughts, or open up more choices for him. Before beginning, check the intention of your questions. Ask yourself, *'Is this question for my benefit, or for my child's benefit?'* If the intention behind your questions is to help you feel better, or to satisfy your curiosity, that's fine, so long as the questions also benefit your child. If there is no benefit *to your child* in your question, then think twice about whether to ask it.

If the conversation is heading in an unresourceful direction, then as a general rule, avoid asking 'why' questions. Answering a 'why' question can be used to justify the negative belief or emotion. For example, *'Why do they pick on you?'* – *'They pick on me because I am such an ugly loser.'* Asking why also takes the conversation straight into the content (or the often very long story of 'he said', 'she said'...). While some content is important, you only need to know the relevant content. If you are not sure what is relevant or not, use a neutral voice to ask your child (depending upon his age):

- Which parts of what you are telling me are the most important?
- What do I really need to know so I can help you best?
- I'm curious, in what way is this relevant to the bullying?

Give your child permission to not know the answer to your questions. If you think your child is saying 'I don't know' as a way of blocking the conversation, go back to building rapport with him, and check your state as well as the state of your child.

Step-by-step: questioning rather than telling

1. Ask yourself, *'Is this question for my benefit, or for my child's benefit?'*
2. Trust that, with your guidance, your child will come up with his own answers
3. Use 'how' or 'what' questions rather than 'why' if the conversation is heading in an unresourceful direction. *'How is that you think they don't like you?'*
4. If your child gives you a lot of details, or a long story, ask him to clarify which are the most relevant parts. *'Of all that you have just shared with me, which part is the most important to you?'*
5. Give your child permission to not know the answer to your questions.

8. How can you respond when your child says 'I don't know'?

You are fully present to your child, you've built rapport, you are listening to the best of your ability and suddenly your child says four *'I don't know'* answers in a row. You wonder if your child doesn't know, or if he doesn't want to answer your questions. If you believe your child genuinely does not know, how can you continue with the conversation? What do you do?

Maybe your child has had enough for now. Check in with him to see what state he's in. Go back and check your original intention or purpose of having the conversation. Check that the conversation is beneficial to your child. Maybe this is a conversation you can come back to later. Have a break, do something else, get something to eat...

If you've checked in and decided to continue with the conversation, you might be tempted to ignore the *'I don't know'* responses and repeat the question, or ask it again in a slightly different way. That might work, but not always. The danger is that you might express your frustration by sighing and walking away, or throwing your hands up in the air and shouting something like, *'Well I can't help you if you're not going to talk to me!'* Hopefully you won't do this!

Children I have coached shared with me common statements parents make which result in them thinking to themselves, *'End of conversation. Goodbye.'* So don't use these responses:

- I think you do know. You just don't want to tell me
- How could you not know?
- Why don't you know?
- If you did know, what would the answer be?

If your child wants to continue with the conversation and *really* doesn't know the answers to your questions, use your rapport skills to match his state of not knowing. You might start by checking your child has given himself permission to not know, and then match him by not knowing too:

- That's fine if you don't know, I sometimes don't know things either
- Sometimes it's great not to know, because it means we get to figure out new stuff
- I don't know either, I wonder if it would help if we talked about it?

If you think your child could benefit from continuing with the conversation, his *'I don't know'* answer does not have to stop the discussion. In fact, Dr L. Michael Hall has documented fifteen different ways to respond to *'I don't know'*.[11] When you figure out what kind of not knowing your child is experiencing, you are one step closer to helping him. Here are eight common kinds of not knowing:

- Has your child given himself permission to know the answer?
- Is your child afraid to know the answer?
- Does your child doubt his answer?
- Does your child not want to know the answer?
- Does your child feel safe enough to know?
- Does your child have any information?
- Does your child have enough information?
- Does your child have too much information?

9. How do you give feedback to your child?

Support your child by providing him with feedback so he becomes aware of how other people experience him. It's a great way for your child to learn about himself. Depending upon how skilful we are at giving it, sometimes our children do not want to hear our feedback! They might experience it as a personal attack, a criticism or even bullying: *'Now you are picking on me too!'*

You can give feedback to your child in a clear and concise way. How would it be for your child if he knew you were not judging, assuming or mind-reading, that you were only stating what you see, hear and feel (and *smell* if you have teenage boys)?

Here are some questions to ask yourself before giving your child feedback:

- What is the intention of giving this feedback to my child?
- Am I in my best state for giving feedback?
- What state is my child in?
- Is this a good state for receiving feedback?

- Am I in rapport with my child?
- Is the feedback I am going to give in sensory-based terms only?
- Have I asked permission to give my child this feedback?

Ask your child for permission! Why would you do that? If you are coming from a state of good intentions, and your feedback is intended to assist your child to become more aware of how others experience him, then you would presumably be coming from a state of care, respect and love. Asking your child's permission (depending upon the age of your child) is a fantastic way to get him on board: *'Would it be okay if I shared something I've noticed about you with you?'*

If your child responds by saying, *'No! I don't want your feedback,'* your next question could be, *'Okay, when would be a good time?'* If your child is still reluctant to talk, use your rapport-building skills and speak generally, not about him directly. For example, *'Some people...'* Or you could tell a story, or use an example of someone you know: *'I once had a friend, and she...'*

10. How can you use sensory-based feedback?

Sensory-based feedback is the type of feedback where you only state what you see, hear and feel. It does not contain your judgements or criticism. Use sensory-based feedback to give your child feedback he understands easily. Because it is simply what you see and hear (and if you want to, you can include what you feel, so long as you own your feelings as yours), it is less likely to be received as an attack on him as a person.

Sensory-based feedback is where you act like a mirror for your child, so he sees himself as others see him: *'I see your arms are folded and your fists are clenched. I see your face is red* and your eyebrows are down. I hear your voice is loud and you are talking very quickly.'

There are no judgements, interpretations, analysis or mind-reading in the feedback. Only what you see, hear and feel. It's specific, honest and free from judgement and interpretation, so it can be useful for the person receiving it.

Sarah's story

Fifteen-year-old Sarah shared that her mum repeatedly told her she is bullied because she has *'a look about her'*. Her mum would say, *'Get that look off your face and smile for God's sake'*. Sarah remembers her mother saying this from when she was about four years old. She shared she has been bullied since kindergarten, and she was *really, really* sick of being bullied.

After establishing rapport using my matching skills, and gaining permission to give Sarah some feedback, I asked her to demonstrate 'the look'. She struggled! She only had a bit of an idea what the look was. She couldn't feel what 'the look' felt like, but she knew she must do it a lot because she always gets bullied, and her mum keeps telling her to stop doing 'the look'.

The week prior to beginning coaching with Sarah, I had been lucky enough to observe her interacting with other girls, including the girls who were bullying her. If I was judging, analysing and mind-reading, I would describe her look as 'snarly', and I could imagine she was sending the message to the other girls: *'Don't talk to me, keep away, and don't come near me'*. Using sensory-based feedback, I gave her the following information:

> *When I was watching you interact with the other girls, including the two you say are bullying you, this is what I saw. I saw*

your eyes were slightly closed and narrow. Your eyebrows were forward, and the frown line between your eyebrows was slightly dinted. Your nostrils looked like they were flared, more than when you smile. Your lips were closed tightly, and your jaw looked tightly clenched. You were looking straight ahead, but slightly downwards, with your eyes fixed on a certain spot in front of you. Your head was tilted slightly forward and downwards. Your arms were crossed in front of you and you were standing at the back of the group, about one metre from the nearest person.

Then I asked Sarah to make 'the look' using my iPad as her mirror. She was then asked to take a photo of herself when we felt she had perfected 'the look'. After much laughter and about twenty photos Sarah studied the picture of her face, and noticed how it felt when she re-created the expression. She then selected a neutral expression (which took just as long!), and noticed how that felt. She was relieved to finally understand what her mum had been talking about. She was genuinely surprised and gratefully received the feedback: *'Wow! That's what I've been looking like all these years?'*

For Sarah, becoming aware of how other people may have interpreted the look was insightful. To reinforce it, we could have asked the girls in her class for feedback about how they experienced being around her.

Share your *experience* of what it feels like to be around your child, so long as you *own* your judgements. For example: *'When I saw you stand up and throw the book across the room and heard you say you hate me, I felt uncomfortable and upset.'*

Firstly, you have given your child sensory-based information about what you saw and heard – he can't argue with that, it's just the facts. Use your matter-of-fact voice. There is no judgement or interpretation or assumption. State the facts as if you were describing what you would have seen if you had recorded it with a camera.

Secondly, you are describing how *you felt* when you were in the presence of your child: 'I felt uncomfortable and upset'. Again, your child cannot argue with that, so long as you are prepared to own your feelings as yours: *'That was my experience, in that moment I felt uncomfortable and upset'*.

By providing sensory-based feedback to your child, you are bringing your child's body language and behaviour to his awareness. This is not about telling him he is wrong or stupid or being silly. Instead, you are letting him know how you experience him when you are around him. You are offering a mirror for him so he can see himself through the eyes of others (for example, his friends at school, the bully, his teachers).

Most people rarely receive sensory-based feedback. You are giving your child a gift.

Chapter summary

- When talking about bullying, most children want their parents to listen and believe them.
- Support your child by listening, remaining silent, and holding a safe space for him.
- If you *truly* listen, your child will often tell you directly how to help.
- To have a supportive conversation with your child it's essential you get yourself out of the way.

- To *truly* listen, enter into the world of your child. Imagine you are him.
- Leave your judgements at the front door and listen for *your child's* meanings, understandings and map of the world.
- For face-to-face communication with your child, it's best to be in rapport. Being in rapport helps your child feel comfortable with your presence, and the conversation.
- Remaining non-judgemental allows you to fully hear your child.
- Give yourself permission to not have all the answers.
- *'I don't know'* doesn't have to be a conversation killer.
- Support your child by providing him with feedback so he becomes aware of how other people experience him.
- Pre-framing, or setting the scene before you begin the conversation, is a useful method of preparing your child to receive feedback.
- Sensory-based feedback is where you act like a mirror for your child so he sees himself as others see him.

Moving forward

In this chapter we have covered many different concepts on communicating with your child. Take the time you need to start implementing these strategies, and seeing what fits for you and your family.

In the next chapter we explore how your child values or devalues herself – whether she does or does not esteem herself. Before you roll your eyes, know that I offer you a *new* way of thinking about self-esteem, as well as an approach you can offer your child. We turn self-esteem inside out, and shake it all about!

6

Self-esteem inside out

Years ago a mother whose teenage daughter was the target of serious bullying shared with me, *'She was such a bubbly, happy, confident girl but the bullies destroyed her self-esteem'*. Back then, I wondered to myself if the mother was talking about self-esteem or self-confidence. Was it possible for her daughter to be bubbly, happy and confident and have no self-esteem? If she had self-esteem, could bullies 'destroy' it? Like the mother, I had more questions than answers. If only I'd known then what I know now. And that's why I'm sharing this information with you.

In this chapter we explore:
- What is the difference between self-confidence and self-esteem?
- What is self-confidence?
- What is self-esteem?
- What does your child believe about self-esteem and bullying?
- What is the step-by-step self-esteeming process?

What is the difference between self-confidence and self-esteem?

Let me share my personal story. I was a quiet, shy child.

Throughout my childhood adults told me I needed more self-esteem. I would try really hard to *get* it, whatever it was, because I knew I needed more of it. I knew that if I had enough of it, I would be happy, confident and popular. I used athletic achievements and academic results to be *good* at something. I thought that would 'give' me self-esteem. Yet it didn't.

As a young adult entering the workforce, various bosses would pull me aside and tell me I needed *more* self-esteem. I wondered what they were talking about. It wasn't until I was thirty-four years old that I finally began to understand what self-esteem was, how I could 'get' some, and when I had enough of it. And I'm happy to report that at age forty, I have it! It was right in front of my nose all along!

Most people do not have a clear understanding of what self-esteem is, or how to get more of it. But we all know we need it. Parents are advised repeatedly to give, raise, increase or build their child's self-esteem without being told what self-esteem is, or the process of achieving that. In recent times, parents are being advised by some experts to be careful not to give their children *too much* self-esteem! Talk about confusing! (Later in the chapter we will explore how it is impossible to *give* your child too much self-esteem.)

Many experts, too, appear confused. At a lecture I listened to a parenting guru spend an hour explaining to the audience the importance of self-esteem in children. When I asked him specific questions about the process, his response was, *'Self-esteem is a mystery'*. Hmm. Maybe I should have asked for my money back!

Driving my children to school one morning, I nearly crashed my car when a radio host suggested to listeners they purchase their daughters a sewing machine so they could, *'Increase their self-esteem by doing something they are good at'*. Oh, pleeease! I had the radio station's talkback number on speed dial but couldn't get through. The message I wanted to get across to listeners was, *'Being good at something doesn't automatically mean your children will esteem themselves'*. And there was a whole lot more I wanted to say – that's why I wrote this book.

What is self-confidence?

A distinction we make and use in the field of Neuro-Semantics is the difference between self-esteem and self-confidence.[12] Most people confuse self-confidence (feeling confident in our ability to perform a particular skill) and self-esteem (our value and worth just for being born). Let's explore self-confidence:

- Self-confidence is very much about what you *do* – your performance
- Self-confidence is a feeling about your ability to achieve a certain task in a certain context
- Self-confidence comes in degrees from high to low. Since it's based on your past experience, you can rate yourself. For example, you can rate how confident you feel about performing a task on a scale from zero to ten
- Your level of self-confidence can vary greatly in different situations. For example, I feel very confident about my ability to drive a car to and from work and not very confident about my ability to drive a car in the middle of Rome in peak-hour traffic
- You can have too much self-confidence. You can feel you can do something when you cannot. When your self-confidence is not based on reality, or on your past experience, it is false

Most people are worried about having too much self-confidence. Coming across as cocky, big-headed, arrogant or a know-it-all is something most people want to avoid for themselves, and their children.

What is self-esteem?

Self-esteem is how we value ourselves. Most people talk about self-esteem as if it exists, but it's not a tangible thing. It doesn't exist physically. We can't hold self-esteem in our hands. It's a process, a verb, a doing word. It's something we *do* to ourselves. We *esteem* ourselves by valuing ourselves and considering ourselves as worthy.

Esteem, when we apply it to ourselves, refers to *our own* sense of personal value and worth. If other people consider us as valuable and worthy, we refer to this as 'other' esteem, or external esteem. Many people esteem themselves conditionally. But unconditional self-esteem occurs when we value ourselves and consider ourselves as worthy for being born, because we are human.

These are some of the comments made by many adults who, in their fifties or sixties, realise they have been chasing external, 'other' esteem while trying to fulfil their need for unconditional self-esteem: *'Why aren't we teaching this stuff in schools?'* And *'I wish someone had taught me this when I was fifteen. It would have saved me decades of unnecessary pain.'*

Some adult coaching clients have even burst into tears when they discover they can esteem themselves. Others experience a sense of relief: *'You mean I don't have to keep doing all this stuff anymore? I can esteem myself whenever I want?'*

Yes!

If you aren't already esteeming yourself, you don't have to wait any longer! And you don't have to wait for the education system to start teaching this information to your children. Start *now*. How?

Begin by being open to changing the way you think about self-esteem. Allow yourself permission to read this chapter and try it on, experiment, and see how it fits for you.

As we clarify the difference between esteeming ourselves and feeling self-confident about our ability to perform a certain task, let's also clarify the difference between esteeming ourselves unconditionally and esteeming ourselves conditionally.

If you esteem yourself *unconditionally* you believe in your value and worth as a human being without question. You have a solid sense of innate worth and dignity. You have unconditional love for yourself. Even when you stuff up and make *huge* mistakes, you still know you are valuable as a person. You know you are more than your behaviours, your stuff-ups, your achievements and your performance. You consider your value, importance and significance as a person is a given. Sounds good, doesn't it?

If you esteem yourself *conditionally*, you believe you must earn the right to be worthy. Your value and worth is *conditional* upon meeting certain criteria. You strive to achieve things to prove your worth to yourself and others by constantly doing and achieving (because you *need* to). You might end up being a high achiever or successful, but you will still feel like you are endlessly chasing your tail, trying desperately to feel good about yourself – only it doesn't last long. You are only as good as your last performance. Off you go chasing your tail again! Sounds exhausting, doesn't it?

I invite you to reflect upon your own approach to esteeming yourself. Do you esteem yourself conditionally or unconditionally? In all my years of coaching, I have found only a handful of clients, including children, who esteem themselves unconditionally. Most people, in my opinion, create conditions or criteria that prevent them from esteeming themselves. Their conditions or criteria might be physical, material, spiritual and so on.

Why do we do this to ourselves? I believe the reason is that we simply don't know any differently.

Some common examples of conditional self-esteem include, in the client's own words, *'My self-esteem will go up when...'*:

- I lose twenty kilos
- I own that car, house, investment property
- I'm on top of my game, I've got my act together, I'm more organised
- I have finished my degree, Masters, PhD
- I have a thriving, multimillion dollar business
- People like me; *everyone* likes me *all* the time
- I am the perfect friend, spouse, mother, daughter, father, son, boss, employee, sister, brother, boyfriend, girlfriend (everything to everyone all of the time!)

Melissa's story

Melissa, aged in her early twenties, requested I coach her because she wanted 'higher self-esteem'. After exploring her beliefs about self-esteem and discovering some conditions she placed upon herself, she surprisingly found she was reluctant to let go of her belief, *'I'll have higher self-esteem when I weigh sixty-five kilos'*. She wanted to keep that condition.

Melissa did not appear above her healthy weight range. In her map of the world, she couldn't esteem herself if she weighed anything over sixty-five kilos. Her decision to esteem herself was completely conditional upon her weight.

> *Things will be better when I lose weight. I'll feel better about myself. I'll be happier, more confident and outgoing. If I esteem myself now, when I'm this fat, I'll blow out to the size of a whale. No, it's better to keep feeling bad about myself until I lose the weight.*

When I repeated her words back to her so she could hear them again, she burst into laughter as she realised what she'd said. Melissa realised she was afraid to let go of her condition that she must be a certain weight because she believed she was using it as motivation to lose weight. When I asked her how she thought this was working, she explained:

> *I thought feeling bad about myself would motivate me to lose weight. But now that I think about it, I haven't lost any weight since the start of the year. Actually, feeling bad about myself makes me eat more!*

Then she joked (and I had tears rolling down my cheeks from laughing with her):

> *It sounds so silly when I say it out loud and pull it apart. Like I'm going to get up every morning, hop on the scales and go, 'Yep, I weigh 64.9 kilos I can feel good about myself today', or 'Nope, 65.1 kilos, NO SELF-ESTEEM FOR ME TODAY, BARGE ARSE!*

If you discover you have a condition or criteria you are reluctant to give up or let go, ask yourself these questions:
- What are the benefits of keeping this condition or criteria?
- What is keeping this condition or criteria costing me?

You will know if your child esteems herself conditionally or unconditionally by listening to how she talks about herself. The language your child uses to describe herself usually gives you a good indication of whether she values herself unconditionally or if she values herself based on certain criteria. For example, she may describe herself as hopeless, or a loser when she doesn't perform as she had hoped. Or she might talk positively about herself as a *person* when she performs well.

Behaviour is also a good clue. Children who try to gain their sense of value and worth through their achievements are often afraid to try new things in case they fail. To them, failing at something not only means they can't do that particular task – to them it means they are *a failure as a person.*

If you think your child esteems herself conditionally, don't panic! By the end of this chapter you will have a clearer understanding of how to help your child.

Justin, aged sixteen, describes his self-esteem criteria:

Before coaching I truly believed I was nothing unless I had certain brands of clothes, the latest iPhone, a certain haircut, and no pimples. And money. I thought I would be popular if I had lots of money. Now I know it's not those things I need. Esteeming myself unconditionally has freed me up to be myself. The funny thing is people seem to be warming to me more now.

And Macy, aged fifteen:

I was amazed at how many different criteria I had. I had to weigh a certain weight, wear certain clothes and be in a certain group of friends before I thought I was worth anything. Once I realised I didn't have to do those things, I'm much happier with who I am as a person.

Your child's decision to esteem herself unconditionally doesn't occur in degrees of high or low. If your child has even one tiny, little condition she must meet before she can value herself unconditionally, her value and worth *is conditional*. (It's kind of like saying you're a little bit pregnant – either you are or you aren't.)

If your child is esteeming herself unconditionally, she can't partly esteem herself or esteem herself some of the time. To help your child understand that unconditional esteeming can't occur in degrees, stop describing self-esteem as high or low. This makes it a lot easier to get your head around. For older children, use the terms 'esteeming yourself unconditionally' or 'esteeming yourself conditionally'.

If your child esteems herself conditionally, it's like she is riding a roller-coaster, and experiencing the highs and lows of how she feels about herself. She experiences the highs when she is meeting all her conditions – she feels great about

> *To help your child understand that unconditional esteeming can't occur in degrees, stop describing it as high or low.*

herself! But as soon as she fails to meet even one of her conditions, she experiences the lows of believing she is less valuable, and worthless.

You can help your child get off the self-esteem roller-coaster by encouraging her to esteem herself unconditionally. Your child making the decision to esteem herself unconditionally is an all-or-nothing choice. She either values herself just for being born, or she doesn't. Therefore, it is impossible for your child to have 'too much self-esteem'. (Remember, it's a process, not a thing.)

When first learning about esteeming themselves unconditionally, some children (especially teenagers) confuse it with self-confidence. They worry if they esteem themselves unconditionally they will get a big head, be full of themselves or – shock, horror – *'people will think I love myself'*. Of course this is not what esteeming yourself unconditionally is about. Esteeming yourself unconditionally allows you to be human: to make mistakes, be vulnerable, try new things and fail at them. It does not make you cocky, arrogant or full of yourself!

What does your child believe about self-esteem and bullying?

Many children believe they have 'low' or 'no' self-esteem. Some believe this is the reason why they are bullied, while others believe they have low self-esteem because of being bullied. Once they realise esteeming themselves is a process they 'do' to themselves, they understand no one can take their self-esteem. They can esteem themselves even when someone is trying to bully them.

I feel excited for them, as I know they will use this knowledge for the rest of their life. Would you like that for your child?

It is useful to explore with your child how she thinks about her value and worth and bullying. For example, nine-year-old Isabella believed the following:
- Kids with no self-esteem get bullied
- I'm being bullied
- I have no self-esteem

Isabella believed the bullying had to stop before she could 'have' self-esteem again. She also believed that if she 'had' some self-esteem, the bullying would stop. It's understandable how Isabella felt stuck in her bullying experience. She couldn't see a way out until she started thinking about self-esteem in a different way.

So far in this chapter we have explored what self-esteem is, and how you can encourage your child to esteem herself. Now we turn our attention to you and *your* concept of self-esteem. Take some time to consider these questions:
- What do you believe about esteeming yourself unconditionally?
- Do you have permission to esteem yourself unconditionally?
- What will this mean to you? To your child?
- What impact does esteeming yourself have on you as a person? As a parent?
- Who are you as someone who esteems themself unconditionally?

Did you discover anything about you and how you think about self-esteem? Did you become aware of anything, or have you become aware of something since the beginning of this chapter?

Maybe you are like many people who believe 'I've always had low self-esteem. It's just the way I am.' Maybe you've been told that all your life?

How can you change your beliefs about self-esteem? How would *you like* to think about self-esteem?

Have you made the decision to esteem yourself, to value yourself for no other reason than you are here, on earth, that you are human? Are you ready to make that decision? Consider the following question:

Have you made the decision to value yourself even when you believe you have failed, let people down, made massive mistakes, and stuffed everything up?

In Chapters Three and Four we explored our ability to make certain thoughts true for us. We can choose to say, 'YES!' to them. We take the thought, '*I am valuable just for being born*', and say, '*YES IT IS DEFINITELY TRUE!*' to it as we make it a belief. As we confirm this thought as true for us, we send messages through our body via our central nervous system and we feel we are valuable just for being born.

Imagine being able to say *'yes'* to statements such as:
- I have value and worth just for being born
- My value is a given
- I choose to esteem myself unconditionally

When you say *'yes'* to a belief, you are also saying yes to the positive, useful value and benefits that belief brings with it. If you

find value, meaning, significance and importance in esteeming yourself unconditionally, the belief will be compelling and appealing to you, and more likely to stick. Ask yourself:
- What is important about choosing to esteem myself unconditionally?
- What will esteeming myself unconditionally mean to me as a person; as a parent; and my ability to help my child?

What is the step-by-step self-esteeming process?

The first step towards esteeming yourself unconditionally is to understand the distinction between esteeming yourself and feeling confident in your ability to perform a particular task. Re-read the start of this chapter until you *know* you understand it. Understanding the difference makes the self-esteeming process a whole lot easier!

The next step is to understand the difference between esteeming yourself conditionally or unconditionally. It's the unconditional self-esteeming you are after. Check there are no conditions or criteria you need to meet. Well, there is one: you are human, and you've already met this one! *Whoo hoo!* Congratulations! As a human, you already have innate value and worth.

The third step is to check you have given yourself permission to esteem yourself unconditionally. Do you have permission to love yourself unconditionally and consider yourself as precious just for being born?

The final step is to make the decision to value yourself unconditionally. Decide you are valuable and worthy just for being born. It's a yes or no decision – maybes or sometimes won't work for this one.

If you have completed the four steps, you are ready to start the process of bringing acceptance, appreciation and awe to yourself. Do that by following the Meta-Stating Self Process.

In his book *The Crucible*, Dr L. Michael Hall documents a process for esteeming yourself unconditionally, the Meta-Stating Self Pattern.[13] As an adult, you can use this process on yourself, or alternatively, have a qualified Meta-Coach take you through it. I use this process in a modified way with children as young as seven. We make it a game, and have fun with it. My experience is that children will enthusiastically and eagerly bring acceptance, appreciation and awe to themselves if the process is presented in a fun and positive way.

Step One: Create a solid sense of self by accessing the states of acceptance, appreciation and awe.

Think of something you have chosen to **accept.** Whatever it is, it used to annoy, bug, frustrate or upset you. It can be something small. Examples might include the fact that no one in your family except you replaces the toilet roll, or sometimes your internet connection crashes. But now you can say in a neutral voice, *'Oh well, it's just the way it is. No point carrying on about it. Just deal with it and move on.'* As you think of accepting your own simple example, notice your voice, breathing, posture, gestures and eyes. Notice how you 'do' acceptance, and see if you can feel it in your body right now, while you are reading this book.

Now think of something you *really* ***appreciate.*** Again, choose a simple example. Maybe you love it when your friend calls you just to say hello or gives you an unexpected thankyou gift. Or when someone asks you how they can help out when you are under the pump. Notice again how you 'do' appreciation, and see if you can feel appreciation in your body right now, while reading this book. Notice your voice, your breath and your posture. What are the eyes of appreciation?

Let's turn it up another level. What are you in *awe* of? Is it the feeling of holding a newborn baby, or taking in the amazing beauty of nature? What leaves you speechless? Maybe you even hold your breath. Again, notice your physiology as you step into awe right now.

Step Two: Step into each of the different states of acceptance, appreciation and awe. Use the simple example of each one to help you feel the feelings. Imagine you have a dial or remote control and can *turn up* the feelings of acceptance, appreciation and awe. Turn them up now, until you feel them vibrate in every cell of your body.

Step Three: The next step is to take those feelings of acceptance, appreciation and awe and *apply them to yourself*. The following are some examples of statements you might feel comfortable to try on (although it's better to come up with your own, unique language that's meaningful to you): *'I accept, appreciate and am in awe of myself because I am human, a member of the human race.'*

If you are religious, you might like to connect with your particular God/s: *'I accept, appreciate and am in awe of myself. I am made in God's image and likeness.'*

If your connection is to a higher self or the universe: *'I accept, appreciate and am in awe of myself. I am a child of the universe. I am made of star dust, the same materials that make up the heart and soul of the universe.'* (I love that one by Dr L. Michael Hall.)

Step Four: As you apply acceptance, appreciation and awe *to yourself as a person,* imagine moving through life esteeming yourself unconditionally. How would life be different for you? For your child? Can you think of some situations or contexts where esteeming yourself unconditionally would make a big difference to you? Can you imagine the you who esteems yourself unconditionally? How does this sit with you?

Amanda's story

Amanda, a forty-year-old woman, never esteemed herself. After years of identifying herself as someone with 'low' self-esteem (her words), she was excited when she learnt she could esteem herself unconditionally. She wanted to start esteeming herself *now*! She eagerly made the decision to unconditionally value herself. Amanda was clear about the difference between self-confidence and esteeming herself. She understood the difference between conditional and unconditional self-esteeming. She understood it all – *in theory.*

Amanda's between sessions task was to uncover any conditions she placed upon herself. When she returned for her next coaching session, she was confused and frustrated. I asked her questions about the process she used to value herself, and it all seemed fine: *'I explored all my conditions and criteria. I did all that. I decided I no longer needed any of them. I valued and esteemed myself all day, every day, but I still don't feel any different...'*

Then I asked her one simple question: *'In what way, if any, do you devalue yourself?'*

After an initial silence, tears flowed down her face as Amanda became aware of the many ways in which she devalued herself.

She realised she constantly criticised herself and called herself 'stupid' or 'an idiot' for the slightest indication of imperfection. She had been unaware of how often she did this, but as she reflected upon it in the coaching session she realised it wasn't just once per day, she did it at least once every hour! Amanda had told herself she was useless every day since she was a child. Now, aged forty, she wanted to change that. Together we celebrated her new awareness. Now she was aware of her pattern, she could change it.

Although Amanda was actively valuing and giving herself worth, she was sabotaging and undoing all her valuing by her incredible ability to devalue herself. In what way, if any, do you devalue yourself? Maybe you devalue yourself by allowing others to treat you poorly. Maybe you don't take ownership of your personal powers. Maybe you take on the role of the martyr and constantly put the needs of others ahead of your own needs. Maybe this is a pattern for you. If it is, until you are aware of your behaviour and recognise it is a pattern, change will be more difficult.

As you explore saying 'YES!' to an empowering belief, notice how you feel it in your body *as true for you*. This is part of the Meta-Stating Self Process. To make a sustainable change in the way you think about esteeming yourself, or to esteem yourself if you never have before, you need to repeat this process many, many times until it feels right for you. It may be you need to repeat the belief you wish to embody hundreds of times until it settles and feels right, feels consistent and normal – until your response is 'of course that's true for me'.

> *'I have worth just because I am.'*

Esteeming yourself unconditionally is a journey. There is no magical switch or on/off button that instantly takes you from conditional to unconditional self-esteeming. It's unlikely to happen overnight, but it will happen as you consistently make the decision to value yourself and acknowledge your own worth, rather than base your value on meeting your conditions.

The process of consistently esteeming yourself unconditionally involves deciding to value yourself in *all* contexts, situations and experiences, no matter what life throws at you. The goal is being able to say to yourself, *'Self, you know what, even though X, Y and Z happened to me, even though I have been successful in many ways, and have failed miserably in some areas of my life, I am still valuable because I'm alive. I have worth just because I am.'*

Helping your child explore and become aware of how she thinks about self-esteem and bullying is vital in her understanding of her bullying experience. Ask questions to help your child explore how she has 'mapped' her beliefs about bullying. Sometimes, just knowing *what* she thinks helps a child to make sense of how she is feeling. Sometimes older children want to know *why* they think a certain way, although this is not a requirement for moving forward.

Make it fun!

With younger children I will often use a large piece of paper, and together we scribble or draw all their beliefs and rules about bullying and esteeming themselves. And, of course, we make it fun. We draw silly faces and use colours and symbols. We pretend we are detectives solving a mystery, or we're searching for hidden treasure, where the children's 'rules' are the treasure. We make a treasure map!

If your child is older she might roll her eyes at your babyish suggestion to do some drawing. Use a whiteboard (this is much more grown-up!) and ask her direct questions. Remember, you are listening for *her* rules, *her* map of the world, not your own. Use your rapport building skills to get yourself out of the way and to listen in a non-judgemental way. (The process for doing this is described in detail in Chapter Five.)

Below are five steps to get you started.

1. Clarify the language
What words does your child use to describe self-esteem and bullying? If she uses the word *self-esteem* as a noun (a thing which exists), then stick with that. If your child is older and you think she is capable of understanding that self-esteem is actually a 'doing' word, use the language *esteeming yourself.* Using words such as value, worth, love, precious and important are fine too. It is helpful to use the words that are meaningful to your child. For example, you might describe 'unconditionally' as 'no matter what'.

2. Clarify her understanding
Check in with your child by asking her what *her words mean to her* – not to correct her, but to understand her. Ask with a touch of curiosity:
- What do you mean by the words 'no matter what'?
- When you say 'low self-esteem', what do you mean? How low? Low in what way?

- When you say you need to get some more self-esteem, how do you think you could get it? What do you mean by 'get' it?

3. Ask explorative questions

Once you have entered into your child's world and have an understanding of *her* meanings, ask:
- What do you believe about esteeming yourself and being bullied?
- What does being bullied mean to you?
- Can you say, 'I am *Unbullyable* and I choose to value myself'?

Some beliefs you might listen for include:
- I was bullied so that means I *must* not have any self-esteem
- I have no self-esteem because I was bullied
- Being bullied took away my self-esteem

4. Make it visual

Draw, write, scribble or paint what your child shares with you. It doesn't matter what it looks like, so long as it is meaningful and fun for your child. Relax! This is not about analysing the drawing. The point of the exercise is for your child to get all their thoughts out of their head and onto paper. You are helping her to step back and see how she has 'mapped' self-esteem and bullying. You are being a mirror for her, so she can decide if she wants to keep this way of thinking or change it.

With younger children I ask them to draw a picture of themselves in the middle of the page. If they won't, I will often draw them with a silly face, their tongue hanging out, crossed eyed or fangs etc. As I ask questions, we add to the diagram. For example:

With older children I'll often do the writing myself. I'll write as fast as they speak. Usually we start by writing the word at the bottom of the page or whiteboard and putting a semicircle around it. Then we work upwards. I ask them: *'What do you believe about self-esteem? And what else? And anything else?'* Then I'll ask them what do they believe about their first answer, and keep working up from there.

5. Invite your child to reflect

Invite your child to step back and consider what was drawn or written. I ask children to physically step back when they are doing this. I might say something like, *'Wow, look at all the great information here! As you look at it from over there, is there anything you notice about it? Is this how it is for you? Is there anything that's missing you would like to add?'*

This is an opportunity for your child to take a look at her thinking from a different perspective. Is there anything she would like to change? Can she scribble or draw those changes now? Does she want a fresh piece of paper to draw her new way of thinking about how she esteems herself? Give your child time to think. Silences are great for this.

Some children stick their work up on their bedroom wall. One fifteen-year-old boy I worked with carried his A4 diagram around with him in his school diary and would get it out and look at it in class. Let your child do whatever works for her. Let her process it her own way, so she can esteem herself; she doesn't have to earn it through her achievements or 'get' it from someone else. If you do that for your child, you have given her the most wonderful, incredible gift which lasts a lifetime!

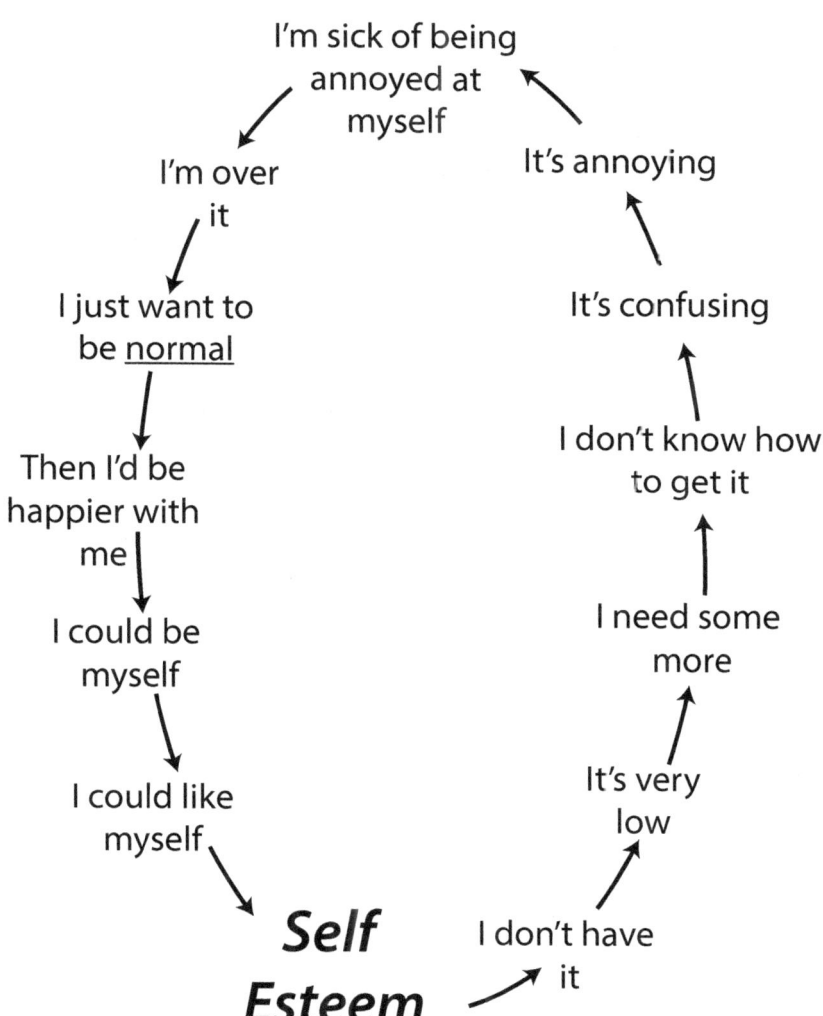

Now you have a greater understanding of the esteeming process, let's explore the most effective way of explaining this to your child. Of course the easiest way is to apply it to yourself. Start to notice how you speak to yourself when you make mistakes: *'I'm such an idiot for forgetting to buy milk…'*

Becoming aware of the language you use to describe esteeming yourself unconditionally when you talk with your child is paramount. Language has such a huge impact on how your child thinks about herself, and her value and worth. Imagine saying to your child:

- I love you just for being born
- You are precious for being you
- You are already awesome because you are human

As you increase your awareness of how you express esteeming, also notice how your child expresses it. As you step back to reflect upon your child's language, ask yourself the following questions:

- Can your child separate her behaviour from herself as a person? Or does she personalise her performance – for example, *'I failed my maths test, I am a failure'*?
- Can your child fail miserably at something and that is okay with her?
- Does your child know she is more than what she does? She is more than her achievements? She is more than being good at something?

Chapter summary

- Self-confidence is very much about what you *do*, your performance.
- Self-confidence is a feeling about your ability to achieve a certain task in a certain context.

- Self-confidence is completely contextual. As you practice the skills, you gain experience and knowledge, and then you feel confident you can do something.
- Self-confidence comes in degrees from high to low. Since it's based on your past experience, you can rate yourself. For example, you can rate how confident you feel about performing a task on a scale from zero to ten.
- Your level of self-confidence can vary greatly in different situations.
- You can have too much self-confidence. You can feel you can do something when you cannot. When your self-confidence is not based on reality, or on past experience, it is false.
- We *esteem* ourselves by valuing ourselves and considering ourselves as worthy.
- We *esteem* ourselves by valuing ourselves. *Esteem* when applied to ourselves, refers to *our own* sense of personal value and worth.
- Your child's decision to esteem herself unconditionally doesn't occur in degrees of high or low. If your child has just one, tiny little condition she must meet before she values herself unconditionally, her value and worth *is conditional*.
- To help your child understand that unconditional esteeming can't occur in degrees, stop describing it as high or low.
- Help your child get off the self-esteem roller-coaster by encouraging her to esteem herself unconditionally.
- Esteeming yourself unconditionally allows you to be human, make mistakes, be vulnerable, try new things and fail at them. It does not make you cocky, arrogant or full of yourself!

- You can't *give* anyone self-esteem. As a parent, it is impossible to *give* your child self-esteem.
- You can esteem yourself by using the Meta–Stating Self Process.
- Esteeming yourself unconditionally is a journey. There is no magical switch or on/off button that takes you instantly from conditional to unconditional self-esteeming.
- Helping your child explore and become aware of how she thinks about self-esteem and bullying is vital in her understanding of her bullying experience.

Moving forward

Have you digested all the information in this chapter? Give yourself the time you need to be sure the difference between self-esteem and self-confidence is clear to you. Once you know the difference between conditional and unconditional self-esteem, you can see clearly how it relates to bullying. Your child's decision to esteem herself is based upon her ability to make that decision. And she uses her *personal powers* to decide.

In the next chapter, we explore your child's sense of personal powers, and how it is relevant to his experience of someone trying to bully him.

7

The power to choose

Imagine having the power to choose how you respond in any situation, circumstance or experience. It sounds great, doesn't it?

What if you could teach your child he has power within him? Imagine if you could support your child to be power-full, rather than power-less.

In previous chapters we explored how to support your child to interrupt the bullying experience by exploring his *beliefs* and *self-esteem*. This chapter provides you with *another* way in which your child can interrupt and disrupt his bully experience, by changing how he thinks about power and challenging his belief that someone has 'power over' him. In this chapter we explore:

- What can we be aware of when talking about power?
- What does power have to do with bullying?
- What are your personal powers?
- How can you own your personal powers?
- Who wants responsibility when they can have POWER?
- What is the Power Zone process?
- How will you know when your child is taking ownership of his personal powers?

What can we be aware of when talking about power?

Sometimes we experience situations where it *seems* like we have no choice. If we experience many of these situations, we may come to genuinely believe that we have no choice. Yet we do.

We choose the meaning or label we attach to the event, situation or experience. We choose how we think about it, what it means to us (if anything) and how we feel about it. We choose to change the way we *think* about it to change the way we *feel* about it.

Some people react defensively when I offer the statement, 'You have the power to choose how you feel'. They accuse me of 'blaming the victim': *'You sound like you are saying it's my child's fault he is being bullied.'*

I understand what they are saying because it took me a while to get used to that idea too. In fact, I would argue with people and defend my choice! *'Why would I choose to feel so miserable? As if I would choose to feel sad!'* Sometimes I would defend myself, *'You are blaming me! Saying it's my fault!'* Now I understand that what was missing was my awareness of my personal powers and my ability to choose. I genuinely did not know I had any choice in how I felt.

So, to clarify, I'm most definitely not laying blame on the targets of bullying because they are not aware of their personal powers. What I'm promoting is the concept we all have the power to take something that happens 'out there', external to us, and give it the meaning we choose. Then we have the power to choose how we think and feel about the meaning we give it. If we don't know we have this power, we may think of ourselves as powerless when we are not.

What does power have to do with bullying?

Many definitions of bullying include the term 'power imbalance', or a statement like *'someone who has power over the victim'*, without defining what they actually mean by 'power'. I have never heard a child describe a bully as having power over him. Most children keep it simple by saying something like, 'Being bullied *makes* me feel scared/angry/frustrated/depressed and there is nothing I can do about it.' For children, part of being bullyable is the belief a bully *makes* them feel something, by a look, a comment on social media or spreading rumours about them.

Adults tend to talk about power in the following way: *'bullying is when someone has power over another'*, or *'bullying is when someone who is more powerful intimidates someone who is less powerful'*. Of course there are people who hold positions of power, such as your boss or the CEO of an organisation. Their *position* means they have the authority to make decisions that have an impact on you, but they do not have the power to *make you feel* a certain way about those decisions. Take away their title or position, and they are human beings the same as everyone else.

Many people live their lives feeling powerless, as if they have no power to choose how they respond. If something happens to them, they believe they have *no choice* in how they react or respond to that event. They believe they *have to* feel sad, happy, grateful, angry or upset. They live their life riding an out of control emotional roller-coaster. They feel powerless to take control of their thoughts, meanings, emotions, actions and words.

I hear adults using language that suggests other people have the power to *make* them feel dumb, good, intimidated, nervous or to experience self-doubt: '*He makes me feel like I'm stupid*', '*She makes me feel good about myself*', '*He makes me feel so guilty for going out with my girlfriends that I end up having a rotten time*'.

By speaking about power in this way in front of children, what are we teaching them? Are we indirectly teaching them that other people have the power to make us feel something?

Here are some questions to consider:
- Are we teaching our children that if they are being bullied it is because there is someone more powerful than them?
- What do we mean by power?
- Power to do what specifically?
- Powerful in what way?

What are your personal powers?

One of the most important aspects in helping your child choose the way he thinks about bullying is the creation or strengthening of his sense of personal powers. Dr L. Michael Hall describes four personal powers:[14]

1. The power to choose what you think/believe
2. The power to choose how you feel
3. The power to choose what you do or don't do
4. The power to choose what you say or don't say

Your personal powers are your ability to respond. Your response-ability is made up of these four personal powers.

You are always responding in some way. You have the power to respond by speaking, feeling, thinking and behaving. You *own* and have *choice* in how you respond, which means you are also accountable for your words, emotions, thoughts and actions. Let's explore each of these in detail.

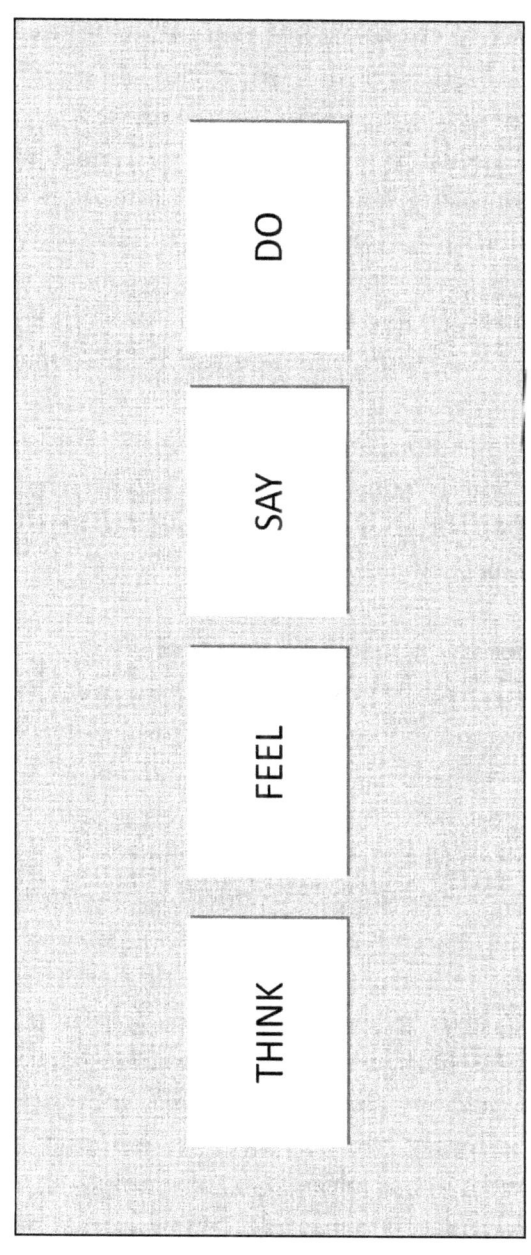

1. The power to choose what you think/believe

Isn't it great you have the wonderful ability to think and believe? Your thinking allows you many things: pondering, reflecting, focusing, remembering, problem solving, creating, fantasising, learning etc. The internal world of your thoughts is private, yours to use as you please. While other people may trigger your thoughts, no one *makes* you think or believe anything. They may invite you to think about things in a different way, but ultimately you decide what you think and believe.

You *own* your thoughts. No one changes your mind without your permission. No one forces you to believe anything against your will. You, and ultimately you, have the power to choose what you think and believe.

2. The power to choose how you feel

The second of your private powers is the power to choose how you feel: your emotions. You are able to feel a wide range of emotions: love, hate, lust, anger, joy, happiness. You have the power to choose how you feel. This power is influenced by your power to choose what you think and believe.

Many people have difficulty understanding they can choose how they feel. Parents often give the example of having no choice but to feel extremely angry about the fact their child is being bullied. They believe they have no choice at all.

Part of being human is we have human responses. Someone hurting our precious child will normally motivate us to take action to stop this. When we accept our emotions as feedback, we can use them to our advantage. For example, there are many choices in how you experience anger. In Chapter Nine we explore how you have choice in at least three different ways: the type, intensity and duration of the emotion.

You have the power to choose to accept your emotions or reject them. You can express them, or stuff, bury or deny them. You have another choice – the choice of how you express your feelings. Often, giving an emotion a different name changes how we experience it. For example, Gemma's mum told me:

> *I was so upset about the bullying. I was heartbroken this was happening to my precious child. I was calling it tragic. I was making it a tragedy. Then I thought about it and realised it's not a tragedy. It's disturbing, it's worrying, but it's not a tragedy. I was making it bigger in my mind and how I felt about it by what I was calling it.*

3. The power to choose what you do or don't do

The power to choose your behaviours and actions is also within your control. No one has a remote control to make your muscles move. You decide whether to take action or not, and what action you take. While it may seem like you have no choice, unless someone has physically or chemically restrained you, you have the power to choose your actions.

Many children, especially those aged between eight and twelve years, challenge this idea by using the extreme example, *'If someone held a gun to my head and told me to do something or I would be dead, I have to do it'*. Well, no. You still have a choice. You are still in charge of your arms and legs. The consequence of choosing not to do it is you might be killed, but it is still your choice. The consequence of not doing what Mum or Dad asks you to do is you will get into trouble. Still, it is your choice.

Sometimes adults challenge this power: *'I don't want to go to work every morning but I have to, I have no choice'*. Of course there is always choice. They can choose not to go to work, but the consequence is their income will be reduced, and their standard of living may drop. Their living arrangements would change, they may have to tighten their budget, but it is ultimately their choice whether they go to work or not.

4. The power to choose what you say or don't say

Your words are powerful. You use them to communicate your hopes, dreams, wants, feelings etc. You choose the words, *'I love you'*, *'I'm not going to let myself be treated like this'*, *'Can I help you?'*, *'I'm leaving you'*, *'I'm proud of you'*, *'I'm sorry I was wrong – you were right'*. (Okay, the last one is a bit harder to say for some people!)

You have the power to choose which sounds come out of your mouth. No one can squeeze your vocal chords, move your mouth and simultaneously position your tongue to force words out. It's not physically possible. You, and only you, have the power to choose what you say or don't say.

And what about the power to choose to say nothing? How powerful is it to choose to remain silent, bite your tongue, or not pass on a rumour? You also have choice in *how* you say something, your tone, your timing, and your gestures. Even your breathing! You have choice in all of these.

How can you own your personal powers?

Why would you want to take ownership of your four personal powers?

Some people remain powerless because they don't know about their personal powers. They genuinely believe they have no power to respond. If you choose to claim and own your personal powers, you are responsible for what you do with them. You have no more excuses. You are accountable for the consequences of how you choose to respond. While this may seem scary or overwhelming to some people, it also means you are empowered. Many people *do not* want to claim their personal powers, as it suits them to be able to blame *others*: 'She made me feel angry, so I had to say something, I had no choice'.

Even if people know about their personal powers, some still choose to disempower themselves. Why would they do this? Choosing to remain powerless makes sense according to their map of the world. To them, being powerless has advantages. They blame others, use excuses and complain that it's everyone else's fault. They play the role of the victim or martyr to get their way or avoid doing what they do not want to do. They blame external things, like other people, their family, the teachers, the weather, the government, lack of money, car troubles, and so on. They also blame their own lack of personal power:

- I don't have the guts/patience/energy/motivation…
- It's just not my style to confront people
- I'm not good at speaking/standing up for myself…
- It's just the way I am, it's in my genes, my personality

Just as you choose to own your personal powers, so does everyone else. Have you ever tried to cheer up someone who was happy being miserable? Trying to 'make' someone feel something will only work if they *allow* you to have an affect upon them. It will only work if they choose to be cheered up by you!

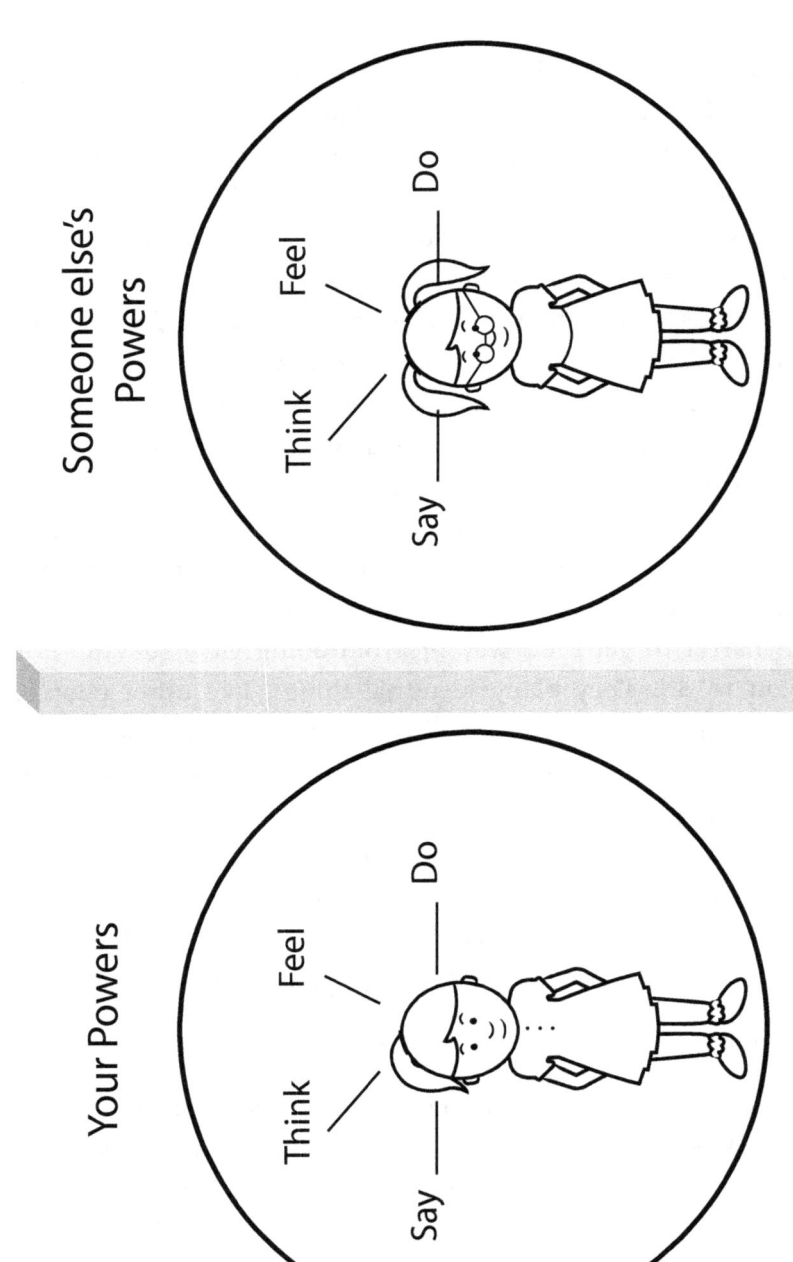

To summarise, we are responsible for how we feel, think, and what we say and do. We are *never* responsible for what another person chooses to feel, think, say or do, even if they try to convince or blame us. We are responsible for our thoughts, feelings, actions and words. We are responsible for our choices in how we respond, but not for the choices made by other people. We do not own the thoughts, feelings, actions or words of other people.

In the field of Neuro-Semantics we make a clear distinction between what we are responsible *for* and who we are responsible *to*.[15] Because you are responsible for what *you* do, say, feel and think, you have a definite boundary. When you try to take responsibility for things outside this boundary, like the feelings, thoughts, actions or words of other people, you may disempower others (if they let you). Many parents ask, *'Hang on, as a parent, I'm responsible for my child, aren't I?'* You have a *responsibility to* care for your children, to give them support, love, safety, security, and teach them to be empowered individuals. But you are not *responsible for* their choices in how they respond. You are not responsible for your child's feelings, thoughts, actions and words.

As a parent you have a responsibility to the rest of society to teach your child how to respect himself, others, contribute and so on, but ultimately your child will make his own choices. You can give him feedback, share with him what you know, be an excellent role model of an empowered person, but it is still up to him to decide how he chooses to respond to you. A gift you can give your child is to encourage him to take responsibility for his own emotions, thoughts, actions and words.

One reason bullying attempts are successful on some children and not others is this: a bullyable child believes a bully *makes* him feel a certain way, and he has no choice in how he feels. An *Unbullyable* child knows he chooses to be upset, or he chooses to dismiss the bullying attempt by believing, '*You can say whatever you want to me or about me, I don't care because I choose how I think about it, the meaning I give to your words, and how I feel*'.

Who wants responsibility when they can have POWER?

As you may have realised, personal powers are actually another way of describing responsibility. I like to think of POWER as responsibility turned inside out. If you try to talk with your child about 'his responsibility', your child might roll his eyes and tune out (instantly!). Seriously, do you think your child wants to talk about *responsibility*? No way! Try talking about (in a loud, excited whisper) THE POWER TO CHOOSE, instead. It's more appealing and interesting. Remember to step into your non-judgemental, curious state and use your excellent rapport building skills.

What if your child chooses *to not own* his personal powers? (Which is still a choice, after all!) While you have a responsibility *to* teach him about his powers, you are not responsible *for* his decisions to own them or not. To explore why your child may not want to own his personal powers, consider the following questions:

- What's in it for him to *not* take ownership?
- What are the benefits? (What if you do?)
- What are the costs? (What if you don't?)
- Has he given himself permission to take ownership of his powers?
- Is this too overwhelming?

What is the Power Zone process?

I have adapted the following process from Dr L. Michael Hall's Circle of Excellence Pattern.[16] Take some time to read and absorb it before inviting your child to follow the process with you.

Begin by playfully introducing the idea of the four personal powers to your child. I do this with children by writing the four powers on square carpet mats and physically stepping (or jumping or hopping or running) from mat to mat (or power to power). You might say something like, *'Hey do you want to play a game about how powerful you are?'* Or for a teenager, *'I just read something that's pretty interesting. Can I show you? Actually it would be easier if we did it together …'*

1. Step into your best state for playing or connecting with your child, and invite him to join you.
2. Ask your child to imagine there is a circle on the ground in front of him, and you imagine your own circle on the ground in front of you. Make sure it's big enough to step into.
3. Ask your child to creatively fill up his circle with his favourite colours, sounds, people, smells, animals and so on. Share with him how your circle looks too.
4. Invite your child to put his four powers into the circle. If it helps, write the words 'feel', 'do', 'say' and 'think' on objects like carpet mats or pieces of paper (although these are slippery to stand on) and put them on the floor inside the circle. Ask your child to place his four powers inside his circle. Now add in the feeling of being powerful – the feeling of having the power to choose what he thinks, feels, does and says. Ask him what he

would see, feel, hear and say to himself as he fully owns these four powers.

5. Before you both step into the circles, ask your child to imagine that when he steps into his circle, he will feel very powerful, see himself as powerful and hear his own powerful thoughts or words.

6. Invite your child to step into his circle, and at the same time step into yours: *'One, two, three, go!'*

7. Once you are inside your circles, invite your child to turn up the feelings, brighten the colours, increase the volume of the sounds, etc. See if he can imagine there is a knob or remote control he can use to amplify the feeling of choosing his thoughts, feelings, actions and words. Invite him to do this until he feels the feeling in every part of his body. Ask him how much he feels this feeling out of ten. Keep asking him to amplify the feeling until he feels like he will burst. (If he can't turn it up to an eight out of ten, ask him what else he needs to add into his circle. Is it permission? Is it liking himself? Is it not caring what other people think of him?)

8. Once he is at least an eight out of ten, ask him to name the feeling: *'What do you want to call this feeling?'* Invite him to step out of the circle and shake off the feeling. Distract him by asking a question like, *'What colour is your schoolbag?'* or any other irrelevant question.

9. Invite your child to step back into the circle, and this time see how quickly he can get the feeling up to a ten out of ten. Remind him to use his posture, breathing, voice etc. To get comfortable and used to this process repeat this step several times, stepping in and out of the circle,

each time feeling the feeling as ten out of ten as quickly as possible.
10. When your child is in the circle and feeling the feeling as ten out of ten, ask him to turn the circle into a bubble by bending down and pretending to pull the circle up over his head so it surrounds him. Ask him to choose the texture of the bubble: *'What does it feel like when you touch it? Is it squishy or hard? Is it see-through? What temperature is the surface when you touch it?'* Ask him to change the bubble until it feels right for him.
11. Invite your child to walk forward, taking the bubble with him. Can he move and the bubble moves with him? Can he step into or out of the bubble whenever he likes? Or does he want the bubble to shrink down and sit behind his ear or go in his pocket ready to use whenever he wants?
12. Invite your child to look through his bubble at the bully. How does it feel to look at the bully knowing he has the power to choose how he responds to the bully? What does it feel like to know he can step into the bubble whenever he wants?
13. Invite your child to imagine when he is next at school or the next time he is near the bully, or the next time someone attempts to bully him (phrase it in whatever language he uses). Invite him to see how he will be different with his power bubble. Ask him to see himself using the bubble in the future, knowing he can step into it whenever he likes, because it is waiting for him to use at any time. What would that be like? How would that help him? Is that what he wants?

How will you know when your child is taking ownership of his personal powers?

One of the indicators a child is starting to take ownership of his powers is when his language starts to change. For example, a bullied child may say, *'They make me sad when they pick on me'*. Once the child begins to learn about his personal powers, his language changes to, *'I choose to feel sad when they pick on me'*, or *'They are still trying to make me feel sad by picking on me, but it's not working anymore because I know I choose how I feel, and those are their words not mine'*.

Maddi's story

Ten-year-old Maddi was bullied by one particular girl in her class for about four months. As well as spreading lies, tripping and pushing her, the bully isolated Maddi by telling her friends not to play with her, leaving her to look for someone to play with each recess and lunchtime. If the bully was away, Maddi's friends would play with her. Sometimes the bully asked Maddi to play, she would be nice for a while, and then suddenly turn nasty towards her. Maddi felt confused and annoyed. She also felt powerless to do anything about the situation. Maddi believed:

- Other people make me feel sad (scared, worried etc.) by their comments
- I can be bullied at school by other kids – I'm easy to bully

Can you see how Maddi's perceived lack of personal power set her up to be bullied? Imagine the big sign Maddi was holding up at school: 'COME AND BULLY ME'. What would Maddi's body posture and voice be like as she tiptoed around the classroom waiting to be bullied?

When Maddi was introduced to the idea of her four personal powers she decided they were pretty good, and she created a power bubble for herself. She chose to own her thoughts, feelings, actions and words. Interestingly for Maddi, she made the distinction the bully's words and actions did not belong to her:

> *The mean stuff she says to me are her words, they are not mine. I don't own them, and I don't want them. Also, I don't let mean words into my power bubble, only neutral or kind ones. I imagine the words floating out of her mouth, through the air, hitting my power bubble and floating right back into her mouth. I see her lips moving and I imagine 'blah, blah, blah' coming out of her mouth.*
> *The most helpful thing has been learning about my four powers. I understand I can't control what she says, but I choose how I react to her. She still sometimes tries to bully me, but because I know what she is doing I just say to myself, 'Here we go again. I know what you are trying to do and it's not going to work anymore', and I give her my best bored look.*
>
> *I think she is starting to catch on I'm Unbullyable now, because she's giving a boy in my class a hard time like she used to give me. I was telling him about his four powers, and to make a power bubble to try to help him because I know he is still bullyable. He is like I used to be.*

Chapter summary

- Many definitions of bullying include the term 'power imbalance' or a statement like, *'Someone who has power over the victim'* without defining what they actually mean by 'power'.
- Many people live their lives feeling powerless, as if they have no power to choose their responses.

- One of the most important aspects in helping your child change the way he thinks about bullying is the creation or strengthening of his sense of personal power.
- You have the power to respond by speaking, feeling, thinking and behaving. You *own* and have *choice* in how you respond, which means you are also accountable for your words, emotions, thoughts and actions.
- You are responsible for your choices in how you respond, but not for the choices made by other people. You do not own the thoughts, feelings, actions or words of other people.
- There is a difference between what you are responsible *for*, and who you have a responsibility *to*.
- One reason bullying attempts are successful on some children and not on others is this: a bullyable child believes a bully *makes* him feel a certain way, he has no choice.
- An *Unbullyable* child knows he can choose to be upset, or he can choose to dismiss the bullying attempt.
- Use the Power Zone Pattern to invite your child to own his personal powers.

Moving forward

This book offers you many resources to help your child. So far we have explored beliefs, communication, self-esteem and now power. Yet there is more. Do you remember how I enhanced the old definition of bullying by adding beliefs and *state*?

The next chapter examines 'state', and how it relates to your child's bullying experience. We explore a step-by-step process of how you can help your child create an *Unbullyable* state she can step into whenever she likes. You can also apply this information to yourself if you choose.

8

An *Unbullyable* state

In this chapter we explore what we mean by the term 'state' and how it relates to your child's bullying experience. We also look at a step-by-step process of how to help your child create an *Unbullyable* state she can step into whenever she likes. We then take that information and *apply it to you* – how you can create your best state for supporting your child.

In this chapter we explore:
- What do we mean by the term 'state'?
- How do we create our states?
- Why is state important within the bullying experience?
- How can you help your child create an *Unbullyable* state?
- How does your child experience you?
- How can you create your best state for communicating with your child?

What do we mean by the term 'state'?
Right now you are in a state.[17] Your state refers to everything about how you are. It's a combination of your state of mind, physical state and emotional state. It can be your nervousness, your hunger, your sense of fun, your boredom or seriousness.

You most likely feel what state you are in at any given moment. Your state is influenced – your thoughts, beliefs, even your posture, affect your state. You are always in some sort of a state.

If the quality of your life is determined by the quality of your states, how much choice do you feel you have over your current states? Do you choose your states, or do you feel they are out of your control? How aware are you of your states?

Take some time to reflect upon what state you are usually in when you are:
- Thinking about your child being bullied
- Talking about bullying with your child
- Hearing your child crying at night because she is being bullied
- Speaking with your child's school teacher/principal/ counsellor about bullying
- Talking about bullying with your spouse/partner/ family/friends
- Reading this book

How often do you change your state? It is estimated that most people experience between *eight and forty* different states per day! Can you count and name your states?

Let's explore your different states:
- How much attention do you generally give to your states?
- What states do you easily notice?
- What state are you usually in?
- Is your usual state a resourceful one?
- Do your most common states energise and motivate you?

Is your usual state a good one? Maybe it gives you energy and motivates you. Or does your usual state zap your energy and leave you feeling helpless, miserable or depressed? Your most common states habituate and drop out of your conscious awareness and become so familiar and comfortable you might not notice them. This is true for both states that are useful, and for unresourceful states. You get to choose the state you want to be in for each situation. You can learn to step into and out of any state you desire at any given time. Sounds good, doesn't it?

How do we create our states?

We create our states using our mind *and* our body. The way we think about things and represent them in our mind affects our body. Think negative, uninspiring thoughts, and you are likely to feel tired, unmotivated and depressed. Think positive, happy thoughts, and you are likely to feel energised and motivated. Being aware of the type of thoughts you think allows you to change your thoughts to positive, useful thoughts and you will begin to feel energised.

Likewise, slouch on the couch, hang your head and drop your shoulders and you are likely to start feeling down in the dumps. If you change your physiology, you change your state. Get up off the couch, lift your head and pull your shoulders back and notice how you feel. Notice your state. Together, your mind and your body create your state.

Why is state important within the bullying experience?

During coaching, many children have shared with me that they feel they have no choice in how they respond to the bully's behaviour. They describe feeling scared, nervous, helpless etc. Some children feel this physically – shaky hands, a hot flush, shaky voice, their mind goes blank. They experience an unresourceful state. They feel they cannot choose how they respond to the bully. For the bullying to be effective from the bully's perspective, your child needs to experience a state that limits her choices in how she responds.

Here's the gold! *Your child can interrupt the bullying attempt.*

Your child can choose the state she experiences when a bully attempts to bully her. The more your child tries this out and experiments with it, and gains confidence in her ability to choose her state, the more her language will change from 'People can bully me' to 'People *try* to bully me, but it doesn't work anymore because I choose the state I'm in when they try. I choose to step into my *Unbullyable* state and refuse to be bullied.'

How can you help your child create an *Unbullyable* state?

Encourage and support your child to create a state in which she chooses to be unaffected by other people's attempts to bully her. I refer to this as the *Unbullyable* state. I use five steps as I help children to create their *Unbullyable* state.

Here are the steps for you to follow:
- Become aware of her current state when being bullied
- Accept any unresourceful states
- Create her new, *Unbullyable* state
- Embody the new state
- Anchor the new state

1. How can you increase your child's awareness of her state?

It is useful for your child to discover what state she is usually in when she's being bullied. By finding out what state she is in, you can help your child to decide if it is useful or not. If using the word 'state' with younger children does not work, find out

the words your child relates to. Use these questions to help your child to discover her state:
- What's it like for you in that moment?
- What do you notice about how your body feels?
- What might you be saying to yourself with your thinking voice?
- What is your body language like?

When you ask your child about the state she is in, keep in mind she may or may not be aware of her state. She may have never noticed, or thought about it. Or she may be able to describe a feeling but not have a name for it. If 'feeling' is a relevant word for your child, you could ask:
- How do you feel when you are being bullied?
- How do you feel when the bully is around you?
- How do you feel right now when you think about the bully?

Remember, we all experience things differently. Your child might not describe a 'feeling'. Your child might see a picture in her mind or hear a voice inside her mind. Whether it's a feeling, a picture, a voice, a combination of these or something else, these are clues as to what state your child is in when she is being bullied. Helping your child be aware of her state is an important step in helping her change her state during the bullying attempt.

2. How can you encourage your child to accept her unresourceful state?

For your child, accepting the state she usually goes into when being bullied is an important part of the change process. Some children will give themselves a hard time about experiencing an unresourceful state: *'I hate it when he makes me feel scared. I hate it that my mind goes blank and I start to shake.'* Help your child to accept her fear and blank mind and shaking legs by reassuring her this response is completely normal. Reassure your child that it is human to experience this response and that she is human! Her brain is letting her know of a perceived danger in order to help keep her safe. She can choose to feel angry and annoyed at herself, or accept the response as normal.

3. How can you encourage your child to create an *Unbullyable* state?

Once your child begins to notice what state she is in and accepts being in this state as normal and okay, she can choose a more useful state. Here are some examples of states children have created as their *Unbullyable* state. Generally they will pick two or three states – for example, *'My best state for being around the bully is relaxed, powerful and curious'*:

relaxed	confident	experimenting
curious	powerful	optimistic
patient	graceful	tenacious
creative	mindful	calm
explorative	courageous	empowered
unruffled	alert	observing

Each child creates their unique state depending upon their age, their past experience, their beliefs and the meaning they give to being bullied. Here are some examples of resourceful states children have created for themselves to step into when a bully *tries* to bully them:

I step into my 'you can't hurt me state'. I choose to feel powerful, tough and strong. Then in my mind I shrink him (the bully) down into a tiny dot and flick him off into outer space.

I use my power bubble to block any of their words getting through to me. I imagine their words coming out of their mouth and bouncing right back at them.

My Unbullyable state is a calm and curious state, and I make their attempt to bully me about them. I ask myself, 'What are they trying to get out of this attempt to bully me?' I say to myself, 'These are their words, not mine.'

My best state for being around her is to expect it. When she tries to bully me, I choose to feel bored. I say to myself, 'Here we go again – BORING!' I add to that, 'I really don't care what you think of me. I'm not interested in what you have to say.' And I look bored. I look her in the eye and then move my eyes past her head and look at the wall behind her or something. I do this to send the message that even the wall behind you is more interesting than this attempt to bully me.

4. How can you encourage your child to embody her *Unbullyable* state?

To put this into practice and make it real, I have included a simple process I use with children during coaching, an adaptation of Dr L. Michael Hall's Meta-Stating process.[18] Use the following process to assist your child to embody her new *Unbullyable* state. Before you begin, take some time to discuss this process with your child, and present it to her in a fun way. You might like to go first and create your own *Unbullyable* state for work, social, and perhaps even family relationships!

1. Ask your child what state she is usually in when she's being bullied or is around the bully. This question is about bringing your child's awareness to the state she is usually in. Ask her to describe it to you, and whether it is a useful state, or if she would like to create a different state:
   - Do you feel anything in your body?
   - Do you think anything in your mind?
   - Are you saying anything to yourself?
   - What is your posture like?
   - What is your breathing like?
   - What is your voice like?

2. Assist her to choose what state she would *like* to be in when someone attempts to bully her or when she's around a bully. Offer your child a menu list if she needs it – for example, *'I choose to feel calm, powerful and strong'*. Ask her to name her *Unbullyable* state:
   - How would you like to be around the bully?
   - How could you be *Unbullyable*? (I have used the term *Unbullyable* in this example. Your child might choose a different name more meaningful to her.)
   - How would you like to choose to feel, think and believe?
   - What would you like to choose to say and do?
   - Would you like to feel calm, powerful, strong, relaxed, curious…?
   - What would you call that?

3. Ask your child what resources she would like to add to her new *Unbullyable* state (a resource is a thought, feeling, idea, belief, value, memory or imagination – for example, '*I choose how I feel*', 'Other people's words belong to them, not me'):
   - Would you like to add anything else?
   - Would you like to add 'I choose how I feel' or 'They used to be able to bully me but they can't anymore because it won't work!'?
   - Would you like to add strength, calmness, curiosity etc.?

4. Ask your child to notice her posture, breathing, voice, and to step into her new *Unbullyable* state now. She does this by remembering the last time she was in it, imagining being in that state, or modelling someone she knows who 'does' that state.
   - When you are *Unbullyable*, what is your posture like?
   - What is your breathing like?
   - What does your voice sound like when you are *Unbullyable*?

5. Ask your child how much out of ten she feels she is in her *Unbullyable* state. On a scale of zero to ten, how much is she in this state right now? If her score is below eight, ask her what she would like to do, think, believe or add to fully be in that state right now. Keep asking her until she experiences the desired state at at least eight out of ten.
   - On a scale of zero (being nothing) and ten (being really), how much are you *Unbullyable* right now?
   - What would you need to do, think, feel or say to be in your *Unbullyable* state right now, right here?
   - Can you do that now?

6. Keep asking your child to increase the intensity of the state: *'Imagine there is a remote control and you can turn this feeling up until it is ten out of ten, until every cell of your body is vibrating with this state'*.
   - Can you turn this up?
   - Can you make it even stronger?

5. How can you help your child create an anchor?

An anchor is a physical gesture your child can use to remind her to step into this state whenever she needs to. Examples of anchors include a breath, a hand movement, or wriggling her toes. A nine-year-old boy I recently coached created the anchor of touching his belly button twice as a reminder to step into his *Unbullyable* state. It was a small gesture, so he could do it in class, in the playground, or wherever he was, and no one would notice. Help your child to choose an anchor that is discrete, not a great, big, weird movement everyone will notice! Once she has chosen her anchor:

1. Choose the physical gesture and invite her to practice stepping into and out of this state. Ask your child to use her physical anchor to access her *Unbullyable* state as quickly as she can. Ask her how much she in the state using the scale of zero to ten. If she is at less than eight out of ten, ask her what else she needs to do, think, feel or believe to get the feeling up to eight or above.
2. Once your child has reached eight out of ten or above, distract her by asking her what she had for breakfast, or what colour her toothbrush is etc. (use a silly example). Then ask her to step into her *Unbullyable* state as quickly as she can. (Make it a game.)

3. Repeat this step about six to eight times, or until your child very quickly uses her anchor to access her *Unbullyable* state. Move around the house and practice in different rooms, standing up, sitting down. Make it as much fun as you can. You want your child to quickly and easily step into and out of this state. (If she is having trouble stepping out of the state, ask her to shake her body or distract her with another silly question.)
4. Ask your child to imagine she is at school (or where ever the bullying is occurring) and to imagine looking at the bully when she is in her *Unbullyable* state. Ask her to imagine stepping into and out of her *Unbullyable* state tomorrow, next week, next month, next year etc. Can she do that?
5. Check that she feels equipped and ready to use her *Unbullyable* state whenever she chooses to. Ask her, *'Would anything stop you?'* If anything could stop her, ask her what other resources she would like to add to her *Unbullyable* state. Keep checking until there is nothing that would stop her, and then ask, *'Will you let yourself use your Unbullyable state?'*

Encourage your child to practice stepping in and out of her *Unbullyable* state. She can do this anywhere, anytime.

This is a powerful tool your child can use to respond to anyone's attempt to bully her. Your child has the power to create her best *Unbullyable* state, give it a name, and then use her anchor to step into and out of it when she needs to. She doesn't stay in the state all day but calls on it when she needs to. Sometimes children will 'store' or 'keep' or 'hide' the imaginary state behind their ear or in their pocket. When they don't need the state, they step out of that state and into another state. Support your child by gently reminding her that her *Unbullyable* state is always there, ready for her to step into.

How does your child experience you?

Now that you have encouraged your child to create her best *Unbullyable* state, let's apply the same process to you.

If you were to see through the eyes of your child looking back at you, and hear through her ears, how do you imagine she experiences you? What does your voice sound like? How are you phrasing your questions and statements? What is your eye contact like? Your posture? Your breathing? Your gestures? Your silences? Does your child experience you as angry, annoyed or frustrated? Or does she experience you as supporting, kind or compassionate?

Your child is likely to be very aware of your state – the state you bring as you attempt to communicate with her. Children sense when their parents are angry, annoyed, anxious etc. Sometimes, outside of our awareness, we display many sensory-based signals and clues about the state we are in.

As Chloe, aged twelve, explained:

Mum would try to talk to me about me being bullied. I knew when it was one of 'those' bullying conversations because her voice would change a bit. She would pretend to be busy doing something. She would try to sound all cool and casual because I think she was nervous. She'd be like, 'Sooooo, how was schooooooool?' I knew she was really asking, 'What happened to you at school today – were you bullied?', but she knew I would get annoyed at her if she asked me that. So I would answer her, like, 'Goooooood. How are youuuuuuu?'

(I must admit I did laugh at Chloe's description of her mum trying to sound cool and casual. It was funny until I remembered doing the same thing with my own teenage daughter, and it suddenly wasn't as funny!)

Let's use the example of creating your best state for communicating with your child (or anything relevant to you helping your child). More specifically, what if you created your best state for communicating with your child *about bullying*?

At times we experience not so helpful states when trying to communicate with our child. I know I do! We bring our own meanings and map of the world about our own bullying experiences. Maybe we experience a negative, unresourceful state and blame ourselves or doubt our parenting skills. We may experience anger, frustration, annoyance and so on. Many people are unaware that, if we want to, we can choose more resourceful, useful states.

You might normally be in a calm, relaxed state, but when it comes to your precious child being bullied, you quickly access a state of angry frustration. The thought of your child being bullied really pushes your buttons! You only have to think about it for a few seconds and you feel tightening in your jaw, chest or hands. Have you tried to communicate with your child when you have been in any of the following states?

stressed	panicky	fearful
tense	negative	anxious
worried	uncertain	furious
confused	angry	upset

How can you create your best state for communicating with your child?

Just as you assisted your child to create her *Unbullyable* state, use the same process to create your own 'best state for communicating':

1. Become aware of your usual state when communicating with your child about bullying
2. Accept any unresourceful states
3. Create your new state
4. Embody your state
5. Create an anchor

Which state would allow you to best support your child? Which is your best state for listening and thinking clearly? For example, let's say you want to change your state from feeling annoyed and frustrated to relaxed and curious as you talk with your child about bullying. If you are being the best parent you can be, and want to support your child, what is the most useful state for you to step into? Consider the following examples of states or choose any other state that works best for you:

relaxed	present	non-judgemental
curious	respectful	reflective
intentional	open	trusting
focused	thoughtful	resourceful
patient	calm	loving
flexible	committed	empowered
confident	appreciative	engaged

If you want to juice up your state, you can create a Meta-State by bringing one state to another to create a combination of states. Let's say you wanted to step into a state of being relaxed

and curious, you could try on *curiously relaxed*. Or you might find *relaxingly curious* works best for you. Create your best states for any situation you like. For example, *'The state I will step into when I am communicating with my child is'*:
- Lovingly accepting
- Calmly supportive
- Quietly confident
- Curiously cautious
- Respectfully firm
- Compassionately engaged

You might like to step into your best state for communicating with your child before the conversation. Like your child's *Unbullyable* state, you don't stay in this state all the time. Create and use your anchor to step into it when you need to, and step out of that state and into another state once you have finished the conversation.

Chapter summary

- Your 'state' refers to everything about how you are. It's a combination of your state of mind, physical state and emotional state.
- Your state is influenced – your thoughts, beliefs, even your posture, affect your state.
- You are always in some sort of a state.
- An unresourceful state can become so familiar and comfortable you might not even notice you are in that state.
- We create our states using our mind *and* our body.
- For the bullying to be effective from the bully's perspective, your child needs to experience a state that limits her choices in how she responds.

- *Your child can interrupt the bullying attempt.* Your child can choose the state she experiences when a bully attempts to bully her.
- Encourage and support your child to create a state in which she chooses to be unaffected by other people's attempts to bully her.
- It is useful for your child to discover what state she is usually in when she is being bullied.
- Once your child begins to notice what state she is in, and accepts being in this state as normal and okay, she can choose a more useful state.
- An anchor is a physical gesture reminding your child to step into her *Unbullyable* state when she needs to.
- At times we, as parents, experience not so helpful states when we are trying to communicate with our child.
- Just as you assisted your child to create her *Unbullyable* state, use the same process to create your own 'best state for communicating'.

Moving forward

Now you have helped your child to create her *Unbullyable* state, and you have created your best state for communicating with your child, we are ready to explore our emotions. Emotions and how your child thinks about them and experiences them are highly relevant to the bullying experience.

In the next chapter we explore how you can support your child to understand and welcome in the emotions he may experience when others attempt to bully him.

9

Empowering emotions

Part of being human is that *we feel stuff*. We are lucky enough to feel emotions, highs and lows, and everything in between. Our emotions play a major role in how we experience life, and the quality of our life.

How we choose to experience our emotions impacts on who we are and how we operate in the world. We can embrace our emotions and use them to support and empower us, or we can turn our emotions against ourselves and live in fear, anger, confusion or frustration.

In this chapter we consider:
- What are emotions and where do they come from?
- What do you believe about emotions?
- How do you experience your emotions?
- What does your child believe about emotions?
- Which emotions are commonly experienced by a bullied child?
- How can you encourage your child to choose his emotions?
- How can you support your child to use his emotions as he moves towards being *Unbullyable*?

What are emotions and where do they come from?

Most people experience emotions as energy, as sensations or 'feelings' in their body. What causes this energy? Put simply, from a Neuro-Semantic approach, emotions are the sensations you feel in your body when there is a difference between what you *think should* happen and what *actually* happens in reality.[19] If you decide the difference is positive for you, then you may experience emotions such as joy, happiness and excitement. If you decide the difference is negative for you, then you may experience such emotions as sadness, frustration and disappointment.

In other words, emotions are information and feedback that there is a difference between the way you think, your map of the world (your hopes, expectations, rules, etc.) and the actual reality of the situation.

If you believe strongly *'no one should ever bully my child'* and, in reality, your child is being bullied, you receive information and feedback in the form of emotions (probably strong emotions!). You feel this energy in your body. You may experience this information and feedback as a tightening of your chest or a sinking feeling in your stomach. Some people *freak out* when they feel an emotion, some feel their emotions in extremes, while others hardly notice them. Consider these comments by parents:

> *Emotions are your body's way of letting you know there is a difference between what you think 'should' happen and what actually happens.*

When I found out my son was being bullied I felt sick in the stomach.

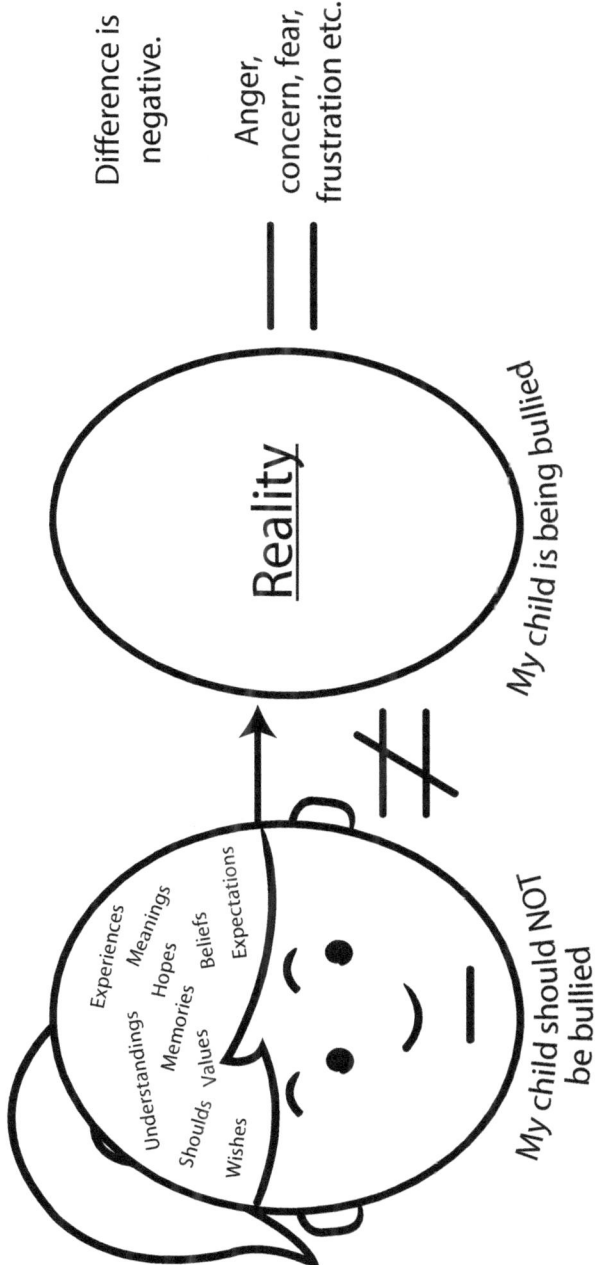

When we had no bullying incidents for over two weeks, my body started to relax. I felt like a weight was slowly being lifted off my shoulders.

- How do you experience your emotions?
- Where in your body do you feel them?
- How aware of your emotions are you?

When how you think things *should* be is confirmed and you *like* the confirmation, or there is a difference you feel *positively* about, you are likely to feel great! When there's a difference, a *positive* difference, you feel emotions such as happiness, delight, joy, love, wonder, surprise, curiosity, celebration, fun, trust, excitement. You feel these when you get more than you expected, or hoped for. For example, you *thought* the meeting with the school principal was going to be stressful, but in reality you felt listened to and you spoke well. There is a difference between your expectation and your reality, and you experienced this difference in a positive way.

When your thinking, your expectations, or your map of the world are not validated and reality is not as you think it *should* be, you may feel threatened. There is a difference between the two, and you don't like the difference. To you, things are *not* as they *should* be; not as you hope, want, believe, expect or signed up for. You may feel angry, afraid, disappointed, frustrated, sad, guilty. Through your emotions, your body is activating your internal alarm system and informing you, *'Things are not right! Something is wrong!'* This information and feedback is helpful as it gives you the opportunity to figure out what the difference is between how you think about something and reality. You can use this information to motivate yourself to take action or to change the way you think.

EMPOWERING EMOTIONS

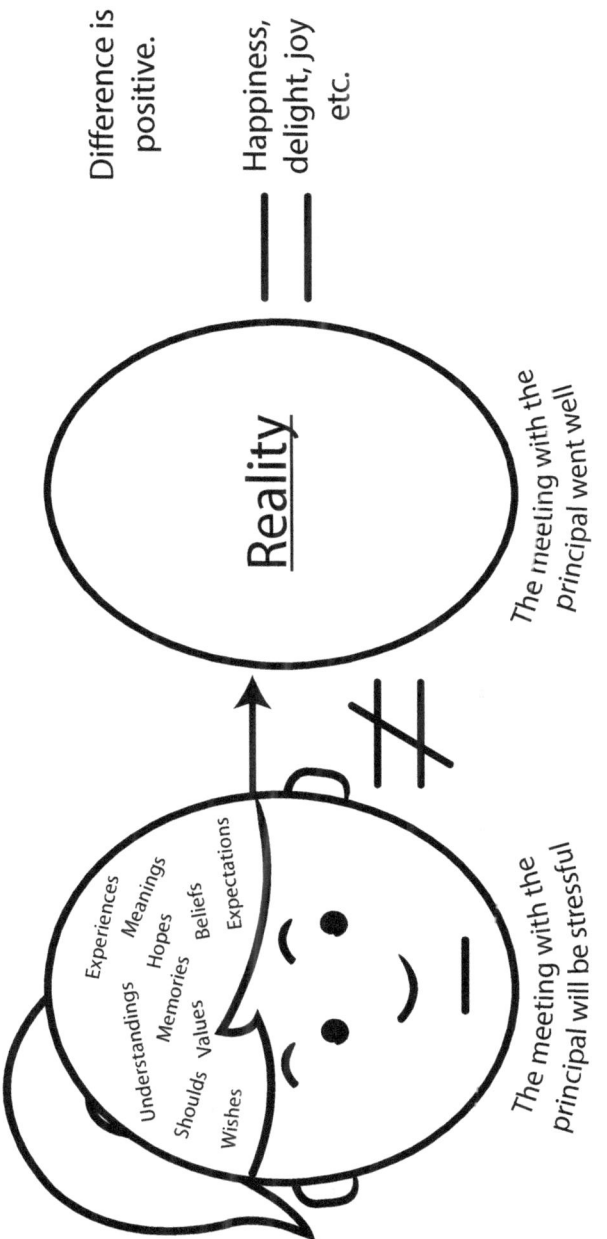

The stronger you choose to believe something, the more it means to you, the stronger the feedback (in the form of emotions) will be if your belief is not reflected in reality. If you give very high meaning to your particular belief, give it high importance and significance, you will feel very strong emotions if your expectations are not what you experience in reality. Your internal alarm system will be ear-piercingly loud! You will be highly motivated to take some action because your belief *means* so much to you.

How you think about the *difference* between your map of the world and reality is important. You can think about the difference positively or negatively – or neutrally if there is no difference. If emotions are information and feedback, you can choose to view them as just that, or you can let them rule you and be a slave to them. Let's explore how *you* experience *your* emotions.

What do you believe about emotions?

How aware of your emotions are you? Consider these questions:
- What do you believe about emotions in general?
- Do you express your emotions or hide them?
- Do you believe if you feel an emotion, it must be true?
- Do you believe you have the power to choose how you feel?
- When you were a child, were you allowed to express your emotions?
- Do you have any *rules* about your emotions?

As you asked yourself these questions what did you become aware of? Did you discover any taboos – any emotions you are not allowed to feel or express? Are you stuffing them away, denying them, or not even noticing your emotions?

How do you experience your emotions?

Do you know someone who cries at the toilet paper commercials on the TV? (You know the ones, with the cute puppies.) This sort of person definitely wears their heart on their sleeve. They feel comfortable expressing their emotions, and might describe themselves as a big sook or say, *'I cry at anything – when I see someone else crying I'll tear up as well'*. They express their excitement, joy, sorrow, and their pain. They may express their emotions through language or song or movement. They openly share how they feel.

In contrast, other people will try to hide their emotions. They hide the fact they are crying, or excited, or nervous and so on. They may hide their emotions so well that others think they do not experience any emotions! People who don't know them might describe them as a 'closed book', or a 'robot', or 'cold'. It could be they don't have permission to feel or express their emotions. They hold on to their emotions, or deny them. For whatever reason (which makes sense to them), they may believe expressing (or even feeling) their emotions is a sign of weakness. To them emotions are dangerous, bad or taboo.

Another consideration is the containment of emotions. Some people experience their emotions affecting all areas of their life. For example, if they have a fight with a loved one in the morning before they leave home, they may take those emotions with them to work. They consider the rest of their day ruined. If they are angry about their child being bullied, their anger spills over into other areas of their life. They may feel they are ruled by their emotions, and believe they have no choice in how they feel as they react to things happening 'to them'.

How do some people seem to manage their emotions, keep their composure and stay in a resourceful state? These people feel their emotions, but contain them to the specific situation, person or event. They have choice. If they have a disagreement with someone, they have the ability to put any emotions to the side and continue to function for the rest of the day. They don't let their emotions affect other areas of their life, unless they choose to. They feel their emotions as distinct. In addition, they choose how they feel, the type of feeling, its intensity and how long they feel it for.

If you were to think back over your life so far, in general, how much choice did you have in how you experienced your emotions?

Why do many people suffer from emotional pain and turmoil? The answer is, they do not accept their emotions as information and feedback. Instead, they *turn their emotions against themselves.* They judge their emotions as 'bad', rather than useful information. They hate their anger. They avoid their disappointment. They fear their love. They experience guilt about their pleasure. It makes sense then, to deny, avoid or make taboo their emotions. They do not have permission to feel these feelings, and they certainly do not accept, appreciate or welcome them in as useful!

The way in which we respond to our child being bullied depends upon our meanings and beliefs. Some parents experience anger, fear and frustration. If you were not aware your child was being bullied, how you responded when you found out is *important to your child*. This is especially true when *your child* shares what is going on for the first time. Unfortunately, many children do not tell their parents any further information about the bullying because their first experience of telling them was not a pleasant one!

Below are some descriptions of how parents felt about their child being bullied. Ruby's mum explained:

> *I felt responsible. I felt like I had failed, that I did not give my daughter the confidence and self-worth she needed. I felt guilty she had to go through it when it could have been avoided. I questioned my parenting skills. I felt anxious and I didn't feel confident about dealing with it. I was over-thinking it. I've sought help to try to make sure it doesn't happen again. And if it does, my daughter will have the tools to deal with it.*

And Amber's mum talking about Amber's dad:

> *I was an emotional wreck, crying and carrying on. My husband was more the silent type. Because he was mainly silent about it, I thought he didn't think it was a big deal. Yet he recently told me he was so worried he lost three kilos when our daughter was being bullied. He's a bloke's bloke, a big strong man. This has been devastating for him.*

Sometimes parents choose not to share the fact their child is being bullied with other parents. As a result, they often suffer in silence. Kim's mum:

> *I thought maybe my daughter was somehow causing herself to be bullied. Then one day I mentioned to her friend's mother she was having trouble with the bully. The friend's mother looked at me in horror and said, 'I thought it was just my daughter.' I was relieved our two girls were both being bullied. Then I felt guilty for feeling relieved. I felt sad it was also happening to my*

daughter's friend. I wished we had spoken sooner so we could have supported our daughters and each other more. It was a lonely experience.

Be assured your response to learning about your child being bullied – the way you feel and think about your child being bullied – makes sense given your map of the world. Ask yourself, *'Is my response helping me to support my child?'* It makes no difference who you are or what you do, as a parent it is understandable to want to protect your child and keep him safe and happy. While running a workshop on bullying for teachers one of the senior staff members shared:

As a teacher, I know all the theory – I have been trained in how to deal with bullying among students. I've been dealing with bullying among students for years. As a parent, when I found out my son was being bullied, I was completely irrational. I was furious at the boy doing the bullying and his parents. I wanted to go straight around to his house and belt him!

What does your child believe about emotions?

Like you, how your child thinks about emotions impacts on how he experiences them. Maybe your child has rules, *shoulds* or taboos about his emotions. It could be that your child is denying his emotions. Is he engaging in emotional eating, drinking, substance abuse or self-harm as he tries to deny his emotions? (If he is, seek immediate professional help.) Or maybe he is so emotional he's difficult to live with, and your family tiptoes around him in fear of upsetting him. How can you find out how your child thinks *about* his emotions?

1. Awareness of emotions
Start by asking your child awareness questions:
- How are you feeling right now?
- How happy out of ten are you feeling right now?
- How do you know? What tells you? Can you show me?
- Can you show me how you do sad, happy, excited, nervous?
- Do you get butterflies or funny feelings in your tummy?
- What do you call that?
- What other feelings do you get? How do you know?

2. How does he think about his emotions?
Ask your child what he thinks about emotions:
- Are you allowed to have these feelings?
- Do you like that feeling?
- Which is your favourite?
- Do you *have* to feel that feeling or can you choose to not feel it?
- Are you allowed to feel angry, sad, frustrated? Are other people allowed to feel angry, sad, frustrated?

3. Check in on your child's map of the world
Through questioning, listen for any clues about how your child experiences and thinks about emotions. Listen for his rules – for example, *'It's not okay for me to cry at school'*, or *'Feeling angry is bad'*. Listen for these things to understand your child, rather than to correct him. Your role is to be a mirror for your child. Repeat back his exact words. If you don't agree with his rules, use a sentence such as, *'So for you, feeling angry is bad...'*

Which emotions are commonly experienced by a bullied child?

Most children have what society would consider as healthy beliefs about bullying: they believe bullying is wrong, unfair and bad. When their beliefs about how they *should* be treated are not reflected in reality, they receive information and feedback in the form of emotions to let them know something is not right, or not as they think it should be according to their map of the world. Sometimes they don't know what to do with these feelings. Often they don't know what to call these feelings. They may even believe it is better not to say anything in case adults think they are 'mental', 'crazy', or 'losing it'.

Your child experiences a range of emotions in response to his bullying experience. In addition to the common emotions such anger, fear, frustration and resentment, some children will also add shame or embarrassment. For example, they may feel guilty about stressing out their parents. Reassure your child that his emotions are absolutely normal and he is not 'mental' or 'crazy' or 'psycho'. If he is old enough, explain to him emotions are useful feedback and information, and he can decide what to do with them. Reassure him that he is more than his emotions.

Eleven-year-old Tim explained what it was like for him:

He would hurt me a lot by what he called me. I would cry at night because I felt scared and worried. It was hard for me to get to sleep. I was worrying about what he was going to do to me next. Then I would get angry because he was probably fast asleep and I was the one still awake at midnight worrying.

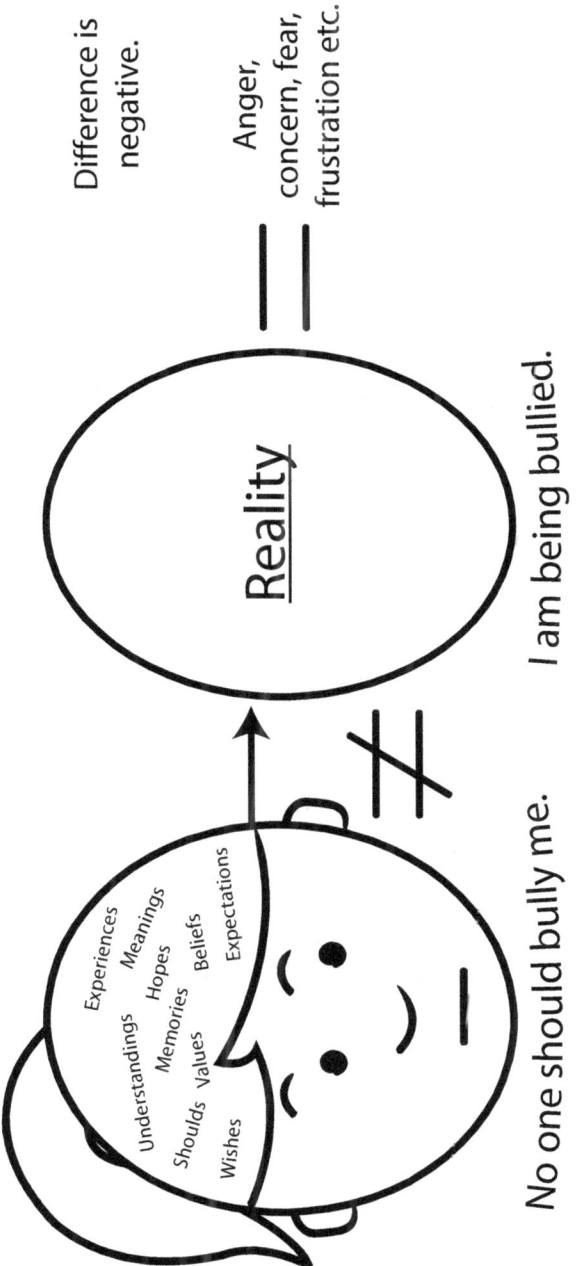

Abbey, aged seven, describes feeling worried and uptight in the classroom:

> *At school I feel like I need to get this feeling out of me right now or else I won't be able to do my schoolwork. Sometimes I want to run away from school.*

Harry, aged eight, explained:

> *That day when I finally went up to him and grabbed him by the collar and told him to back off was the best day ever. I felt so powerful. I felt like I was Superman and he was a little ant. I was proud. I was happy. I was excited I finally did it.*

Rachel, aged twelve, talks about fear:

> *Kids get bullied and then they are afraid to come to school because they are afraid of being bullied again.*

It is common for children to feel absolutely exhausted by the bullying experience, especially if it has been ongoing and they can see no end to it. Support your child by acknowledging when he is feeling tired, and accept how he is feeling without making judgements. Reassure your child that feeling tired is a very common symptom of being bullied. Check that your child does not have a health condition that is causing the fatigue (or he's staying up until 2am on Facebook!). Support your child by providing him with a safe and peaceful home environment.

Tania, aged sixteen, explained:

> I was tense all day at school and I just wanted to come home and crash. I needed to be somewhere where it's not pressurised. I needed a safe environment to escape to. I just needed to relax and for it to be calm. I could feel safe and secure at home. Luckily I had that. I guess some kids don't have that.

How can you encourage your child to choose his emotions?

Maybe the idea of choosing your emotions is a foreign idea or concept, and you are thinking, 'I can't choose how I feel!' If this is the case, see if you can give yourself permission to 'try on' the idea for a few minutes. Imagine yourself having the ability to choose how you feel by choosing the type, intensity and duration of your emotions.

1. Type of emotion

Let's say you are feeling sad about something. Do you know you can choose the 'type' of sad you feel? For example, if you were to bring anger to your sadness, you would have *angry sadness*. If you were feeling sad because you experienced a disappointment, you might feel *disappointed sadness*. If you were feeling sad because you were lonely, you might call the feeling *lonely sadness*. The point is, *you* get to choose what type of sad you feel. And if what you are feeling is not helping you or your child, you get to choose again!

It's like taking an emotion – 'sadness' or 'anger' – and adding another emotion to it. You can feel angry about your anger, or calm about your anger, or frustrated about your anger, or afraid of your anger. You can choose the type. If you have felt angry,

frustrated or fearful about your child being bullied, you may have chosen to feel:
- angry anger
- frustrated anger
- fearful anger

In the past, did these types of emotions help you to support your child? If you still wanted to feel angry (because anger can be a very useful emotion), but wanted to be more helpful for your child, you could choose to feel:
- resourcefully angry
- purposely angry
- calmly angry

To help your child understand this concept, simplify it depending upon his age:
1. Hold out one clenched fist in front of you and say, 'I choose to feel angry'.
2. Place your other hand on top of your fist and say, 'And calm. I choose to feel angry and calm. I choose to feel *calmly angry.*' For a very young child say, 'I choose to feel angry and calm at the same time.' The important thing is that he is learning he has a choice in how he feels.
3. Ask him to feel *calmly angry* throughout his whole body. What is the posture of calmly angry? What is the voice and the breathing?
4. Repeat this process with other emotions – for example, the first clenched fist is 'happy', then add 'quietly' with the other hand: 'I choose to feel *quietly happy.*'

2. Intensity

Did you know you can choose how much you feel an emotion? Have you felt emotions in degrees, or on a continuum from zero to ten? Have you ever experienced five out of ten angry? Or do you tend to jump straight to ten out of ten angry? It's common for bullied children to experience 'all or nothing' emotions: they either feel *not at all* angry or *very* angry, with nothing in between. If they feel even the slightest bit angry, they jump straight to ten out of ten angry in zero point zero seconds!

If you think your child might experience his emotions in extremes, use the following exercise to encourage awareness and flexibility. The aim of this exercise is to increase your child's awareness (especially for younger children), and to encourage flexibility in his thinking and feeling. Make sure you use language appropriate to the age of your child.

1. Step into a state of fun, curiosity and exploration and invite your child to 'play' with you. Do you have permission to play and be silly?
2. Use your rapport building skills and check your child has permission to explore his emotions with you:
    - Does he have permission to talk about his emotions?
    - How could he give himself permission if he wanted to?
3. Choose any space where you can walk along an imaginary line of about three metres. Use a basketball or tennis court, your living room, the length of your kitchen etc.
4. Ask your child to choose an emotion (for this example I have used happy, but you can do this for any emotion), and walk along the imaginary line making one end zero out of ten happy and the other end of the line ten out of ten happy. Ask your child to stand with you at the ten out of ten happy end, and describe how he 'does' happy. You could ask (in a non-judgemental, curious voice):

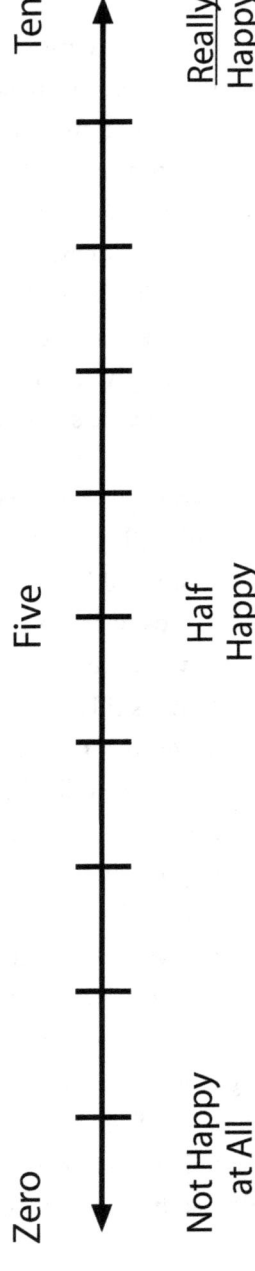

- When are you here?
- Can you imagine being here?
- What does it feel like in your body?
- How does your skin feel, your stomach, your chest?
- Can you show me the posture, your face, your eyes, your jaw?
- What is your breathing like when you are here?
- What does your voice sound like when you are here?
- What kinds of things would you say to yourself inside your head?

5. Invite your child to walk with you to the other end of the line, which is zero out of ten happy. Ask him the same questions. Be silly. Have fun with it!
6. Invite your child to walk with you in the middle of the line. Repeat the same questions.
7. Invite your child to move somewhere else on the line – for example, two or five or seven out of ten – and use the same questions for that place on the line. The aim is for your child to feel the different degrees of the emotion. Changing his body posture, facial expressions and voice is important. There should be a noticeable difference in these between zero and ten out of ten. Other differences will be more subtle.
8. Ask your child some awareness questions:
   - Where are you normally (usually, generally, most of the time) on this line?
   - Do you like it there?
   - When is it useful to be there?
   - When is it not useful?
   - Is that where you want to spend most of your time?

9. Encourage your child to move around the line.
    - Where would you like to be?
    - If you wanted to, can you move from that spot to a different spot?
    - What does it feel like? What is the posture, breathing, voice?
    - Can you move all around the line when you need to?
10. Celebrate with your child! Tell him how fantastic it is that he can move anywhere on the line: *'Wow! You are telling me you can choose to move anywhere on this line whenever you want to? Fantastic! So you can choose to be one out of ten or eight out of ten or whatever? What's great about that? How is that useful for you? What did you discover, find out, or learn? How could you use this at school?'*

3. Duration

Ask your child if he can decide to stop being angry, or does he have to wait for something to happen? Can your child choose how long he stays angry for? Is it for one minute, an hour, all day? How does he decide on how long he stays angry for? Some children will say they don't know: *'until it goes away'*. This kind of language indicates they don't believe they have any choice in how they experience their emotions. A question to ask is, *'So after dinner, when you have decided to stop feeling angry, what will you choose to feel then?'* You are letting your child know he has the power to choose how he feels.

How can you support your child to use his emotions as he moves towards being *Unbullyable*?

You can encourage your child to choose how he feels by the language you use. Let him know an *Unbullyable* person chooses how they feel. I started teaching this to my children when they were toddlers, but whatever the age of your child, it's never too late to start. The following is an example of a conversation I remember having with my son when he was aged four. He was angry about the Lego tower he was trying to build. I turned to him and said in a neutral voice, *'I see your turned up nose and your eyebrows are forward and down. I hear your voice is louder than usual. I'm wondering if you are choosing to feel angry?'* (Sensory-based feedback, also awareness of how other people see him.)

'Yes I am!'

'Oh, *I'm wondering what sort of angry you are choosing to feel. Is it annoyed angry, useful angry, frustrated angry, sad angry or another type of anger?'* (Type of anger.)

'I'm angry angry!'

'How *much are you choosing to feel angry angry out of ten? A little bit, in between, or a lot?'* (Intensity.)

'A lot! Ten out of ten!'

'I'm *wondering how long you are going to choose to stay a lot, ten out of ten angry angry for. Just a little bit, until morning tea, lunch, dinner, until bedtime?'* (Duration.)

'All day! Until bedtime!'

'Okay, so let me see if I've got this right. You are going to choose to be angry angry, a lot, ten out of ten, until bedtime. Is that what you are choosing?'

'Yes.'

'How *will you* choose *to feel when you choose to stop feeling angry? What will you* choose *to feel instead?'*

'Happy. Then sleepy.'

'How will you choose *to change from angry angry to happy, then sleepy?'*

'I will smile, and lie down in my bed.'

'Can you show me your smiley face now? Just so I know how you do it. And your voice? What would your voice sound like if you were choosing to feel happy? Can you show me now?'

'Yes.'

Of course now he's a bit older he's not interested in going through this process. I giggle to myself when I sometimes hear him say, *'I'm choosing to be angry angry, ten out of ten, all day until I'm not.'* The point is, he is aware of his anger, and he knows he has choice. He knows nothing can *make* him angry unless he chooses it. As he grows older he will learn to experience degrees of anger, and how emotions are useful information. He's also aware of other people's choices to feel emotions.

As I'm writing this and thinking how clever I am and I definitely deserve a 'Mother of the Year' award, let me share with you something else. I was driving him to kindy (and running late again, late for my 9am meeting straight after the kindy drop-off). I was stuck behind an *idiot* driver, driving about forty kilometres per hour in a seventy kilometre per hour zone, *whose slow driving was making me insane*. A little voice from the back seat innocently asked, *'Mum, how are you choosing to feel about the car in front of us?'* Hmm.

Chapter summary

- Our emotions play a major role in how we experience life, and the quality of our life.
- We can embrace our emotions and use them to support and empower us, or we can turn our emotions against ourselves and live in fear, anger, confusion, or frustration.

- Emotions are your body's way of letting you know there is a difference between what you think 'should' happen and what actually happens.
- When how you think about things is confirmed, and you *like* the confirmation, or there is a difference you feel *positively* about, you are likely to feel great!
- When your thinking, your expectations, or your map of the world are not validated and reality is not as you think it *should* be, there is a difference between the two, and you don't like the difference.
- The stronger you choose to believe something, the stronger the feedback (in the form of emotions) is if your belief is not reflected in reality.
- The reason many people suffer from emotional pain and suffering is they do not accept their emotions as information and feedback; instead, they *turn their emotions against themselves.*
- How your child thinks about emotions impacts on how he experiences them.
- Most children have what society would consider as healthy beliefs about bullying – they believe bullying is wrong, unfair and bad.
- Reassure your child that his emotions are absolutely normal and he is not 'mental' or 'crazy' or 'psycho'.
- It is common for children to feel *absolutely exhausted* by the bullying experience, especially if it has been ongoing and they can see no end to it.
- You can choose the type, intensity and duration of an emotion.
- Teach your child he has choice in how he feels by the language you use.

Moving forward

Let's recall the tools you have so far: beliefs, communication, self-esteem, personal powers, state and emotions. Use all this information to help support your child to become *Unbullyable*. And now I offer you yet another useful topic: movies.

In the next chapter we explore the 'movies' your child plays in the cinema of her mind. We explore why these movies are important and how you can encourage your child to change the bullying movies she is playing if she wants to. It's fascinating stuff and your child will *love* it.

10

Unbullyable movies

'Your child changing the way she thinks about bullying, bullies, and herself as a target of bullying is the most powerful tool she has in becoming Unbullyable.'

This chapter is about the 'movies' your child plays in the cinema of her mind.[20] Using that metaphor, we explore how your child represents the bully and her bullying experience when she closes her eyes. As you read this chapter it will become clear how the movie metaphor works, and how to use it to help your child.

I have included this information for two reasons. The first is that children love it. They enjoy it. To them it is *fun*. And they are good at it. Compared to the adults I coach, most children are faster and more open to this approach. (Maybe it's all the time they spend on screens?) The second reason is that children tell me it works! Often when I ask children to think back to what helped them the most in their coaching program they answer *'the movie stuff'*.

In this chapter we explore:
- How do you create your movies?
- How can you use this information to help your child?
- What are the benefits of stepping out of your movies?

- How can you step into or out of your movies?
- Why are the movies your child plays about her bullying experience important?
- How does your child re-present a bully in her mind?
- How can your child change her movies?

How do you create your movies?

Think about your favourite movie. You have probably watched it more than once. You might even have a copy of it in your DVD collection. You might be able to recall particular scenes and recite certain lines from the movie. You watched it up on the big screen at the cinema, or on your television at home, but right now you can recall certain parts of it in the *cinema of your mind*. You 'play' parts of the movie and 'watch' it without too much effort. How do you do that?

When we watch an 'external' movie, event or experience through our eyes and hear it through our ears, feel it or even taste it, we take this information and 're-present' it in our mind. We have the ability to reproduce an event that happened in the outside world, and 'watch' it again on the screen of our mind. (Sometimes over and over again!) We also use the screen of our mind to recall things, create images, dream, fantasise etc. We are amazing! This ability is fantastic for 'remembering' things that bring us joy and happiness, but unfortunately, we can also choose to re-present events or incidents we consider as negative or bad.

> *We have the unique and wonderful, and even magical, ability to literally re-present what we have experienced in our senses 'on the inside of our mind'.*[21]

Part of the experience of being human is that we are always playing some movie in our mind. It's very common to not be aware of what movie or the type of movie we are playing, yet we are constantly taking information from the external world and representing it as pictures and images in our mind. The interesting thing is that as we do this, we are sending messages into our neurology and nervous system, and we feel these sensations as feelings. We might even call them emotions. This is important, because if we think 'negative thoughts' and play 'negative movies' we begin to 'feel' down, tired, hopeless and so on. When we play happy, motivating, inspiring movies, we begin to feel energised, hopeful and excited.

Another fascinating thing about being human is that we have the ability to get things wrong. Have you been through exactly the same event or incident with another person and afterwards you and the other person recall two completely different experiences? Have you ever watched a movie with a friend (a real movie 'out there') and completely missed a sub plot your friend says was, *'so obvious, I can't believe you missed that!'*?

How is this possible? The answer is your meanings, the way you interpret things, your thinking styles, and what is important to you. These things have an impact on the movies you create. Your experience of reality is not the same as reality, therefore it makes sense your movies could be different from someone else's movie of the same event. (Ask anyone who has been through a divorce!)

In a nutshell, the movies we play in our minds are not an accurate reflection of true reality. So in the process of re-presenting our reality, we generalise, summarise, alter, change, distort and even delete certain aspects.

Can you see the implications for your child as she creates a movie of an external bullying incident? Can you see how two children who are the targets of the same bullying behaviour can experience it in two different ways? One experiences the behaviour as 'bullying' and the other as, *'It was nothing. They were just mucking around.'* The children's different meanings, interpretations, beliefs, expectations, rules, past experiences and so on influence the movie they create of the bullying behaviour.

How can you use this information to help your child?

Firstly, as a parent it helps you to understand why your child is affected by bullying while other children are not. Secondly, the movies your child plays in the cinema of her mind impact directly on how she feels. The movies she plays in her mind have a huge impact on her state, emotions, feelings, behaviour, skills, world view, perceptions, health and life. If your child is lying in bed playing 'bullying' movies over and over, it is actually having a direct impact on her body. Fascinating, isn't it?

Many bullied children describe playing movies of bullying experiences over and over again, as if on auto-replay. This is especially common when they are trying to fall to sleep at night. When I asked eight-year-old Eddie how much he thought about being bullied during his two-week school holiday break he told me, *'Half the time'*. Half of his school holidays were spent thinking about the boy who was bullying him. Eddie said he couldn't help it, he tried not to think about the bully, but he would find himself thinking about him again and again. He believed there was nothing he could do about it.

Fifteen-year-old Bec explained:

> *I just keep going through what happened that day in my mind and going over it and over it. It's like I can't stop thinking about what has happened. I think about what I should have done instead of what I did. I get really upset and angry and then I can't sleep. I'm awake sometimes until two or three in the morning. Mum doesn't know but she did hear me crying the other night. She tried to help by getting me some relaxation music but it didn't help. It's like I can't turn my brain off. Then I'm too tired when Mum wakes me at seven in the morning for school. It's really annoying because then I'm tired all day.'*

As Bec lies in bed playing her bullying movie over and over, her brain sends messages through her central nervous system and she 'feels' the emotions of being bullied. Her brain does not know the difference between what is real and what is a movie, and she feels the feelings of being bullied while lying in her bed at night. No wonder she can't sleep – she's taking the bully to bed with her each night!

Yet Bec doesn't have to play the movie over and over. And she doesn't have to feel the emotions that go with the movie. Bec can learn to step out of her movie at any time. In addition, she can change the way she thinks *about* the movie. It is possible for children of Bec's age and younger to learn how to do this. But firstly (as usual), let's start with you.

Take some time to consider these questions:
- How aware are you of the movies you play?
- As you think about the movies, would you consider them mostly positive, negative, or neutral?
- Are they mostly about the past, present, or future?

- What *type* of movies do you play? Are they action, drama, horror, comedy, romance?
- Are you usually the actor (seeing through the eyes of you the actor) in the movie, or are you in the audience watching you in the movie?
- Do your movies generally energise you, or leave you feeling drained of energy?

Some people say they don't play any movies. It is likely they do, however, they are just not consciously aware of their movies. Movies can flash across the cinema of your mind in two to three seconds. Pictures, images, sights, sounds, sensation, smells and tastes pop in and out of our movies in what seems like a split second. And if we are not aware of them taking place, they are easily missed.

We are in charge of the screenings, yet most of us are not aware of this. Most of us don't do 'movie reviews' of the movies we play, but play random movies, over and over again. We play whatever is in our DVD collection. For most of us there is no quality control, no rating system. Most of the time we have no idea what we are watching because we do not bring it to our conscious awareness.

When we play movies repetitively, the fact we are playing them drops out of our conscious awareness. We don't even know we are playing them. One clue is if we are conscious of our body, and the feelings in our body. When we notice we are feeling stressed or upset by the feeling in our stomach, we can ask ourselves, *'What movie am I playing for me to be feeling like this?'* Our physical sensations are very helpful hints, giving us the opportunity to step back and notice the type of movies we are playing.

What are the benefits of stepping out of your movies?

Why would you want to be able to step into or out of your movies? Imagine being able to step out of movies that result in you feeling bad, and being able to step into movies that result in you feeling good. Well, you can! Whenever you play a movie with you as the actor, your body thinks it's real because it is receiving the signals from your brain as though *it is real*. In his book *Movie Mind*, Dr L Michael Hall explains: *'If you play a trauma scene (yours or someone else's) from within the movie as the key actor of the action, then you will experience more trauma.'* [22]

Can you think of the implications for your child if she is playing her bullying movies with herself as the actor over and over again? What are the implications for you, as a parent, if you repeatedly play movies of your child being bullied? One parent described it as, *'I felt like I was being bullied all over again...'*

When you step out of your movie and be in the audience, or take a different perspective, like as a camera operator, director, editor or producer, you can be an observer to your movie. You can view the movie without experiencing the emotions that go with it. Being able to view the movie from a non-judgemental perspective supports you to re-evaluate it. You can change the way you think *about* the movie. This means we can always step out of the movie we are playing. We never have to feel like we are 'stuck' in a movie.

Not only can we change the viewing perspective, and how we think *about* the movie, we also have the power to change the content. Once we step out of our movies we can change them to more useful, resourceful or inspiring movies, and then step back in. What power we have!

How can you step into or out of your movies?

There are some great benefits in stepping into your positive movies and out of your negative movies. Here are some ideas to help you begin the process. You can, of course, experiment and come up with the technique you feel most comfortable with. The steps include:

1. Awareness of movies
2. Acceptance of movies
3. Changing perspective

1. Awareness of movies

Before being able to step in or out of your movies, it's important to be aware of what movies you are currently playing. Ask yourself questions that result in you actively bringing the movies into your conscious attention. For example:

- What movie am I currently playing?
- What type of movies are they?
- How do I feel when I play these movies?

2. Acceptance of movies

Once you are aware of your movies, and the type of movies you are playing, the next step is to accept them. This may seem or feel strange at first. The reason for accepting them is that it can be difficult to change something you haven't accepted. Fighting against your movies, trying not to play them, feeling bad, annoyed or angry for playing certain movies does not help to empower you to change them. If you notice you are playing what you consider 'negative' movies and you don't want to feel bad, instead of giving yourself a hard time, accept the movie and the feelings. Say to yourself, in your best neutral, matter-of-fact voice: *'Oh, that's interesting. I'm playing a movie about everything going wrong again. I'm noticing the heavy feeling in the pit of my stomach.'*

Or add a touch of curiosity and intrigue: *'I wonder why I play that particular movie whenever I am around her?'*

Can you see the difference between noticing, observing, and being aware of your movies in a non-judgemental, curious way, as opposed to, *'I am such an idiot because I can't stop thinking that! I'm so useless I annoy myself. I should be able to stop thinking that.'*

3. Changing perspective

It is useful to be able to consider your movies from a different perspective.[23] Stepping out of your movie allows you to take on different ways of thinking about it. You can choose to feel different emotions as you consider your movie from a different perspective. You are no longer stuck. Let's practice stepping into and out of movies and to gain flexibility in our perspective.

First position: you the central character

When you are the central character, you are inside the movie looking out through the eyes of you the actor. Look out of your eyes at the other actors. As you are in the movie, you feel the emotions of the 'you' in the movie.

Second position: you as another actor

Now imagine you are no longer 'you the central character' in the movie. Instead, you have stepped out of that role and you are now playing the role of another actor looking at 'you the central character'. Notice what you see as you look at yourself. Notice your facial expressions, your posture, your voice, even your breathing. You are looking at 'you the central character' through another person.

Third position: you the observer

Now imagine you have stepped out of that role and you are someone else on the movie set – for example, the camera operator. Imagine you are recording 'you the central character' talking with 'you' the other actor. Notice what you see as you use the camera to record the movie. How are the two of 'you' interacting with each other? How far apart or close you are? Remember, you are just observing, not judging.

Fourth position: you the director

Now imagine you have stepped back off the movie set and you are standing next to it in the role of the director. In this position you tell the other versions of 'you' what to do. You direct yourself and the other actors inside the movie to act in a certain way. You as the director can ask for more attitude, a different emotion, less intensity etc. You direct the camera operator to zoom in or zoom out in certain scenes.

Fifth position: you the editor

Now see yourself sitting in your editing room. As the editor, you create the movie you want as you cut, delete, zoom in on certain scenes, add special effects and decide on the individual sound tracks. You create whatever movie you like!

Sixth position: you the producer

Now imagine you are sitting in your office in Hollywood. You are the producer, and as the producer you make the decisions that influence everything about the movie. You can change the movie from a horror movie to a comedy, an action or drama to a romance. You set the scene. You choose the type of movie you create. You control how much money and time is invested into this movie, and you decide when it's up to your standard, when it successfully meets your criteria.

How did you go? Were you able to take on the different perspectives of the movie? When it came to creating the movie you want, did you create a blockbuster movie for your mind?

This movie process shows you how you can take control of the movies you create, the movies you act in and the movies you watch. Use all of the roles, from actor to producer, to create resourceful, uplifting, enhancing, useful movies and step into your movie to fully feel inspired and energised.

If we are always playing a movie in our mind, and our movies are always sending messages into our body telling us how to feel, wouldn't it make sense to play great, uplifting, inspiring movies and step into them? What type of movies do you usually play? What categories of movies are in your DVD collection? How big is your 'comedy' collection, your 'drama' collection, your 'what if' collection? Do you need to create some new, positive movies to add to your collection? How often do you refresh your best movies?

What does your DVD collection of all your movies say about you? Would any 'go viral' if you posted them on YouTube? Would you proudly invite your child into your library and show her your collection? Are you a good role model? If not, what would you choose to change? Which movies could you put aside and let gather dust and which ones would you like to watch over and over again?

Now you have thoroughly explored your movies – how they are made, how to step into and out of them, how you can change them, how you watch them from different perspectives – you are ready to support your child to explore her movies.

Why are the movies your child plays about her bullying experience important?

Children who have been bullied will sometimes play the 'bullying' incidents over and over again. It's like they have them on auto-replay. They go over and over the event in their mind, looking for what they may have missed, thinking about what they should have said, could have done etc. Many times, they frame the movies they play as hopeless, horror or drama. Of course these types of movies send signals and messages into their body and they feel stressed, upset, hopeless and scared. Ella, aged twelve, described what it is like for her:

> *I think about her all the time. She's always there in the back of my mind. At school, at home, at dance. She's always there in my head, even in bed at night I'm thinking about what she is going to say about me tomorrow.*

Just as you have your own collection of movies, so does your child. What type of movies do you think your child is playing? If she is old enough to understand, explain the movie metaphor to her. Then take her through the same process you used to explore your movies. Ask her:
- What is your collection like?
- What categories do you have: comedy, drama, horror?
- Would you like to have more or less movies in some categories?
- Which movies are your favourites?

- After which movies do you feel awesome?
- After which movies do you feel down/sad/annoyed?
- Do you want to create new movies for your collection?

How does your child re-present a bully in her mind?

Many children *carry a picture of the bully around with them.* As an eight-year-old girl described: *'I take my bully to bed with me inside my head.'* And a ten-year-old boy said, *'He's in my head all the time, even when I'm watching TV at home.'* Continue to use questions to gain more understanding of how your child thinks about the bully. For example:

- When you think about (the bully), do you see a picture in your mind of him/her?
- Is it a still picture, like a photo, or does it move, like in a movie? (If it is a movie, ask her if she is 'in' the movie like an actor, or out of it like being in the audience. If in, invite her to step out of the movie.)
- Is it in colour, or black and white?
- How clear or fuzzy is the picture of the bully?
- What size is the picture of the bully? Is it the size of the screen on your phone, or a plasma TV, or up on the big screen like at the cinema? Or a different size from these?
- How far away does the picture of the bully seem to you? Close up to your eyes? Off in the distance?
- What shape is the picture of the bully? Rectangle? Round? Square?
- Does the picture of the bully have a border around it? What is the border like? Soft? Hard? Sharp? No border?
- Are there any sounds with the picture of the bully? Your voice? The bully's voice? How loud or quiet? What tone?

- How long does the picture stay in your mind? Do the pictures stay on the screen of your mind for very long, or do they seem to flash across the screen quickly? If you see movies, how long are they?

How can your child change her movies?
Once you have an understanding of how your child thinks about the bully, support her to change the picture if she chooses. Let her know how to step out of the movie or picture (if she is in it) and photoshop it. Invite her (in age appropriate language) to be the director, editor, producer etc. Invite your child to step out of the movie and photoshop her picture of the bully.

Here are the how-to steps for three options your child can use to gain flexibility and resourcefulness when thinking about a bully:
- Changing the picture
- Perceptual flexibility exercise
- Social panorama exercise

> *'When I shrink her down it feels like she isn't there anymore. Then I can listen to the teacher more.'*

1. Changing the picture
The first exercise is not about changing the picture of the bully in a negative or aggressive way.[24] For example, during this exercise, a young child might want to shrink the bully down, throw the bully into a volcano, squash him or her like an ant, or make the bully ugly, with warts and pimples etc. Doing this produces 'negative' movies. And whenever your child plays negative movies, she is sending

messages into her body to feel bad, especially if she has stepped into the movie as an actor.

This exercise is about your child choosing how she *thinks* about the bully. It's about letting her know she has choice, and that she doesn't have to walk around thinking about the bully all day. The key is for her to be aware of the movies she plays when she thinks about the bully, and then know she can choose to change a movie whenever she likes. There is no need for her to feel angry or negative during this exercise, she is just experimenting with the quality and cinematic characteristics of the pictures in her mind. For example:

- If your child says the picture is in colour, can she change it to black and white?
- If the colours are bright, can she dull down the colours?
- If the picture is clear, can she make it fuzzy?
- If the picture is large, or taking up her whole thinking space, can she shrink the picture down to the size of a cinema screen, then a large plasma TV, then the screen on her phone, then the size of an ant, then a pinhead, then a microscopic singular cell organism?
- If she describes her picture as right in front of her, ask her to move the picture to where it feels comfortable. Some children send their picture floating off into the next universe. Others shrink the picture down to a size they feel comfortable with then move it off to the side. It's still there, but they are in control of where it is, and they can *push it out of the way so they can do their schoolwork.*
- Invite your child to change the shape of the picture to whatever she likes – it's about her being in control of her thinking. If the shape she describes is a rectangle, can she

change it into a different shape, like a love heart or a circle or a floating bubble?
- Can your child change the border? Can she make it disappear, go fuzzy or make it out of feathers?
- Invite your child to mute the sound, or even mute the bully's voice. Can your child turn up the volume on her voice and turn it down on the other voices? Would making the bully's voice sound like your child's favourite cartoon character be fun?
- Can your child lengthen or shorten the amount of time she thinks about the bully? How about adding commercial breaks to the movie? Can she fast forward parts of the movie and slow down other parts?

2. Perceptual flexibility exercise

Perceptual flexibility is the ability to see a situation from different positions.[25] Invite your child to close her eyes and guide her through the following steps:

1. What do you see as you look through your own eyes? Can you look down and see your own hands?
2. Now imagine you are me looking back at you through my eyes. Can you see what I see as I look at you?
3. Next, imagine someone else is here observing us. What do you see as you look through their eyes as they look at us looking at each other?
4. Now imagine there is a camera up on the ceiling and it's pointing down at us. Can you imagine what it records?

This exercise is useful in encouraging children to be aware of how others experience them. It helps them notice their posture, their voice, their gestures etc. You may encourage your child to explore how the bully or other children see her through their eyes. This information is useful when discussing body language when she interacts with the bully or other children.

3. Social panorama exercise

The social panorama exercise is useful to gain insight into how your child sees herself in relation to other people, including a bully.[26] Invite your child to close her eyes and create a picture of an open space like a football oval or playground in her mind (she can draw it if she prefers):

1. Invite your child to put herself in the middle of the space.
2. Ask her to describe or draw where she would place people around her. For example, where are her family members, friends, pets, the bully, teachers?
3. Ask your child to notice where she places different people. Is there anyone who is close or far away?
4. Ask your child if she would like to move anyone around. Would she like to move anyone closer or further away? Would she like to try moving anyone somewhere else?
5. Ask her to go ahead and do that now, and to notice how that feels for her.

I have taken many children through this exercise, and while each child is unique, some common themes have emerged. Typically, children will either put the bully very close to them or very far away, like in outer space. For the children with the bully very close, they will often move the bully further away and give themselves some space to breathe. Interestingly, after coaching, children who placed the bully in outer space will bring the bully in closer – but not too close! These children have explained it to me as, 'I don't need to keep her that far away, because she can't bully me like she used to'.

Fourteen-year-old Jaxon explained:

On my oval I had my bully right up in my face. He was right in front of me. So I moved him further away. Then I moved him off to my left. Then I moved my two best mates in closer to me. I had my mum and dad and my brother and my two best mates closest to me. My bully was there but at least I could see my family and friends. It felt good to move him out of my way because he was getting really annoying.

For Jaxon, it felt right to move the bully far away from him. For other children, moving the bully closer helps. For twelve-year-old Beth:

In my first picture my bully was far away, and on my left. I had my family close to me, but my friends were a long way away. I felt a bit lonely. Everyone seemed far away. In my second picture, I moved everyone in, including the bully and her friends. It's not that I want her near me, it's that I have her closer to me because now I have more friends around me. It might sound weird, but I actually feel more comfortable with her closer. I don't have to spend any energy trying to push her away. I am more comfortable with being around her than I used to be.

Chapter summary

- Your child changing the way she thinks about bullying, bullies and herself as a target of bullying is the most powerful tool she has in becoming *Unbullyable*.

- Telling your child to change her behaviour and her words does not work unless she also changes her thinking and what she believes.
- Humans have the unique ability to re-present what we have experienced in our senses on the inside of our mind.
- When we watch an 'external' movie, event or experience through our eyes and hear it through our ears, feel it or even taste it, we take this information and 're-present it' in our mind.
- The movies we play in our minds have a huge impact on our states, emotions, feelings, behaviours, skills, world views, perceptions, health and life.
- Many bullied children describe playing movies of bullying experiences over and over again, as if on auto-replay.
- We are in charge of the screenings, yet most of us are not aware of this. Most of us don't do 'movie reviews' of the movies we play; we just play whatever, over and over again.
- When you step out of your movie and be in the audience, or take a different perspective, you can be an observer to your movie. You can view the movie without experiencing the emotions that go with it.
- Not only can we change the perspective on our movie and how we think *about* it, we also have the power to change the content.
- If we are always playing a movie in our mind, and our movies are always sending messages into our body telling us how to feel, wouldn't it make sense to play great, uplifting, inspiring movies and step into them?

- Many children *carry a picture of the bully around with them*. Once you have an understanding of how your child thinks about the bully, you can support her to change the picture if she chooses.

Moving forward

It's interesting to notice the *type* of movies we play. Sometimes it's possible to see a theme or pattern emerge as we reflect upon the *type* or *kind* of movies, rather than the content of the movies. It's the same for our thoughts in general.

As you think about the type of thoughts you have in one day, do you notice any styles, themes or patterns? This is the topic for the next chapter – your child's thinking styles and how they relate to his bullying experience.

11

Unbullyable thinking styles

Knowing how your child represents things in his mind assists you to understand and communicate with him. When you know your child's preferred style of thinking, you can use *his* language to build rapport and communicate with him. Imagine having the flexibility to go into *your child's* world so he feels listened to, validated, heard, understood and supported. He no longer has to keep repeating himself. To do this, it is useful to be aware of what your preferred thinking styles are, and those of your child. In this chapter we consider:

- What are thinking styles?
- How does your child prefer to process information?
- How are thinking styles relevant in the context of bullying?
- What is all-or-nothing thinking?
- What is personalising?
- What is over-generalising?
- What is discounting?

Firstly, let's look at thinking styles.

What are thinking styles?

Our thinking styles refer to the way we sort, filter and perceive what we pay attention to in the world around us. In this chapter we describe a mixture of thinking styles, also known as Meta-Programs[27] and cognitive distortions.[28] A simple example of a thinking style is that some people will notice the details, while others notice the big picture. If you ask people who love the details how their day has been, they will spend ten minutes telling you all about the details of their day. People who prefer big picture thinking might answer, 'Good'.

How does your child prefer to process information?

We all think differently. We take in information from our external world through our senses and reproduce or re-present it in our minds. Most people develop a favourite or preferred way of doing that. Some people are highly visual and see images and pictures, others use sounds and produce soundtracks, while others process information by noticing how they feel about it. Most people use a mixture of all three ways of processing and representing information, yet we often have a favourite.

To identify your child's preferred style, ask him these questions:
- When you think about someone, do you see a picture of them, hear their voice or feel the feelings?
- When you learn something new, do you like to watch, listen to instructions or try it yourself?

If your child prefers to re-present things *visually*, he may:
- Process and organise his world visually
- Move his eyes upwards when visualising
- De-focus his eyes to imagine things out in front of him

- Like to look at others when talking with them
- Like things to 'look' right
- Use words such as 'see', 'view', 'peek', 'show', 'looks right', 'spot', 'glance'

If your child prefers to process *auditory* information, he may:
- Process and move his eyes with sound
- Move his eyes from side to side when accessing information (as if looking at his ears)
- Have the gift of the gab
- Be sensitive to tones and volumes
- May point to his ear when talking
- Likes things to 'sound' right
- Use words such as 'listen', 'hear', 'sounds right', 'call', 'whisper', 'quiet'

If your child prefers to process *kinaesthetically*, he may:
- Process and organise things by noticing his body sensations
- Move his eyes downwards (as if looking at his body)
- Breathe deeply, talk and move slowly
- Use a lot of gestures
- Like things to 'feel' right
- Use words such as 'touch', 'feel', 'fall', 'struggle', 'handle', 'sense', 'move'

Once you are aware of your child's preferred thinking style, start to listen for your own. You will hear it in your language. Next, match your child by entering *his* world by using his language. For example, asking your highly visual child how he *feels* about being bullied is less effective than asking him how he *sees the big picture* of the bullying he is experiencing. In other words, even if you are a kinaesthetic processer, if your child is predominately visual then use visual language.

How are thinking styles relevant in the context of bullying?

We use different thinking styles in different contexts. For example, the thinking styles your child may use in the safety of your home may be different from the thinking styles he uses at school when another child is attempting to bully him. It's possible for a child who thinks in extremes in other contexts to *bring that thinking style to* his bullying experience. Let's explore four of the most common thinking styles I see in children affected by bullying:
1. All-or-nothing thinking
2. Personalising
3. Over-generalising
4. Discounting

What is all-or-nothing thinking?

If we perceive bullying as a threat to our personal safety, our brains kick into survival mode and we experience a 'fight or flight' response. It's common for us to experience this as 'all-or-nothing' thinking. If we are aware we're doing it, we can question its usefulness, and decide if we want to keep using it or not. We are also aware it is highly likely we are limiting our choices to 'black ' or 'white ', with no grey options. Sometimes all-or-nothing thinking is very useful and at other times unresourceful or limiting in some way.

In my experience in coaching children affected by bullying, I have noticed it's very common for them to think and speak in extremes about bullying. I hear this in their language when they use words such as 'always', 'everyone', 'no one', 'all' etc. For example, Bonnie, aged nine, genuinely believed, *'Everyone is always picking on me'*.

Bonnie was not lying or exaggerating, she really did feel like *everyone* was *always* picking on her, or about to pick on her, *all* of the time. From an observer's point of view it might appear very obvious that not everyone is constantly picking on Bonnie, but it *feels like that for her*. She believes it to be true. Judging or telling her she is silly to think that, or accusing her of trying to gain the attention of others may be experienced by Bonnie as another personal attack, and provide more evidence for her that *'Everyone is always picking on me'*.

How would you know if your child uses an 'all-or-nothing' thinking style in the context of bullying? He may:

- Make circumstances pervasive: 'Everyone *is picking on me* everywhere, all *of the time'*
- Believe things are either this or that, black or white, with no shades of grey in between. Friends are either best friends or enemies
- Be limited in his choices and options. He sees only two choices, 'this' or 'that', with no other possible choices or flexibility in his thinking
- He may experience his feelings in extremes. He may feel his emotions as ten out of ten, or zero out of ten, with nothing in between

If your child thinks in an all-or-nothing style when it comes to his bullying experience, you will hear it in the language he uses. The way your child thinks and speaks about bullying influences how he experiences it. As he describes *'everyone picking on him all the time'* and *'no one liking him'*, this becomes true for him in his mind.

Could it be possible that you are an all-or-nothing thinker when it comes to the context of your child being bullied? Notice when you hear yourself saying or thinking, *'I want my child to be happy all the time'*, *'No one should ever bully my child'*, *'Everyone picks on my child all the time and makes him absolutely miserable'*, *'He is not at all happy at the school'*, *'The school has done nothing'*.

Take a step back to notice how you speak about bullying with your child, spouse or friends. If all-or-nothing language is evident, ask yourself if how you are expressing yourself about the bullying situation is having an impact upon how you are feeling about it. Simply noticing and then changing your language about the situation makes a difference. For example, rather than saying, *'My son is being constantly bullied by a gang of boys and is absolutely distraught'*, try, *'There are three boys who are pushing and shoving my son, at least once per day, as well as making comments to him. About twice per week, he is extremely upset by this.'*

You can help your child create flexibility in his thinking by exploring his map of the world. Do this by being a mirror to him, and reflect back to him what he has just said, and how he has said it. Using your rapport building skills, and together with your child, pull apart and explore his statements about bullying by asking about *exceptions* to the all-or-nothing thinking. Then, with curiosity and wonder, introduce the possibility of some other options besides black or white. Respectfully ask your child:

- Is it 'always' like this, every single time?
- Is there ever a time when it isn't?

- Is there a time when it's 'in between'?
- How much out of ten do you feel anger/sadness/frustrated/lonely?
- Is it ever higher or lower?
- If it isn't X or Y, what else could it be?
- What else could X mean? And what else?

If you listen to your child, you will hear certain words that indicate the all-or-nothing thinking style. Words such as 'all', 'always', 'everywhere', 'every time', 'everyone', 'never' and 'no one' are examples of all-or-nothing language. If you would like to encourage your child to move away from all-or-nothing thinking, introduce continuum language such as 'mostly', 'sometimes', 'a lot of people', 'some people', 'at times', 'the majority', 'a few', 'partially' etc.

Jordon's story

Jordon, aged thirteen, experienced all-or-nothing thinking when he thought about his bullying experience. Jordon also spoke in all-or-nothing terms, saying, 'Everyone *is against me*', '*I get picked on* all *the time,* every day', '*I have had enough of everything*', '*I don't care about* anything anymore'.

When asked what he meant by these comments, Jordon was unable to specify exactly what he meant. Through asking about the exceptions, in a supportive, non-judgemental way, Jordon became aware of his all-or-nothing thinking. He was reassured that during times of stress, or when we feel threatened, it's normal to sometimes 'do' all-or-nothing thinking. Jordon was reassured that his all-or-nothing thinking was a normal response to his bullying situation. As he realised there was nothing wrong with him, and he made sense, he felt relieved!

By bringing this to his awareness, Jordan was able to step back, notice his all-or-nothing thinking and experiment with some slightly different ways of thinking:

'Everyone *is against me*' changed to, 'One *boy is trying to bully me*'.

'*I get picked on* all *the time,* every day' changed to, '*I get picked on* some of the time, not *every day*'.

'*I have had enough of* everything' changed to, '*I have had enough of* his attempts to bully me'.

'*I don't care about* anything anymore' changed to, '*I do care about lots of different things, and there are* some things *I have chosen not to care about as much as I used to*'.

What is personalising?

Personalising is another thinking style common among bullied children. If your child personalises, he takes what someone says or does and makes it about him, even if it's not. This is an example: '*Some girls were whispering and laughing at the back of the classroom. I just know they were talking about me.*'

Targeted bullying directed straight at your child will feel *very personal*. To them, everything *seems* directed towards them, even if it is not. In addition to feeling like they are the target of bullying, some children will personalise *every* comment, gesture and incident. They will take it to heart. It's understandable they experience it as an attack on them as a person, shaking the very core of who they are. As they *personalise* the bullying, the bully's words and actions, they increase the meaning and the affect the comment or action has on them.

If your child is personalising he may:
- Make everything about him, even if it's not directed towards him

- Perceive circumstances and actions of others as targeted towards him, even when not intended or communicated that way
- Not be able to see the world through the eyes of others
- Take feedback personally and use it for feeling bad

If you suspect your child is making things about him when they are not, you will more than likely hear it in the way he speaks about his bullying experience. You may hear him overuse words such as 'me', 'I', 'mine', 'myself', 'I am'. He may focus his attention on his own experience and be unable to view the experience from the eyes of the bully, bystanders, teachers or parents.

There are many ways to help your child if you discover he is personalising the comments or behaviour of the bully. The first is to encourage your child to see himself from a different viewpoint. Ask him questions like:
- If this isn't about you, what or who could it be about? What else? Anything else?
- If you could look at this situation from neutral eyes, such as the eyes of a camera, what would you see?
- Could this be about them, and not about you? How? How else?

Encouraging your child to make the bullying about the bully is also helpful. Ask your child (with a touch of curiosity of course!):
- What if you made this about the bully, and not about you?
- I wonder what is going on in the bully's world that he/she feels he/she needs to try to bully you?

Giving your child information about bullies in general is also helpful. It takes the focus off your child and puts it on the behaviour of the bully. You might say to your child, in an age appropriate way, *'Here's some information about bullies in general. I'm not saying this is about all bullies, but it's pretty interesting'*:

- *You know what? Most bullies are really sad kids who don't know how to be friendly*
- *Lots of bullies don't like themselves very much*
- *They might seem cool and popular, but as they get older research has shown bullies become less and less popular. They might have lots of friends now, but by the end of high school most kids don't like them anymore*
- *Unfortunately for kids who bully, many of them end up with criminal records as adults*
- *Kids who bully are more likely to become violent adults. They also have trouble with their relationships*

Some younger children who start off hating the bully change their opinion after receiving this information. They even go so far as to feel 'a little bit' sorry for the bully.

How about you? Are you personalising the fact that your child is being bullied? Do you consider that your child is being bullied a reflection upon you as a parent? Consider what it means to you that your child is being bullied. When you are having a conversation about bullying with your child, notice if you're making it about you. Are you personalising the fact you are the *parent* of a bullied child? For example, if your child's teacher gives you feedback about your child, how do you respond? Is that response helpful to your child?

What is over-generalising?

So far we have explored all-or-nothing thinking and personalising, and now we add one more to the mix: over-generalising. Remember Jordon, the thirteen year old who used an all-or-nothing thinking style in relation to his bullying experience? Now consider his statements as he over-generalises:

- 'He said he doesn't like me' for Jordon meant, *'No one likes me or anything about me'.*
- 'He said I am annoying' for Jordon meant, *'I am annoying to everyone'.*
- 'He said he didn't want to play with me' for Jordon meant, *'He never wants to play with me'.*

For Jordon, in that moment, he *really, truly* believes no one will ever like him. It's *true* for him, even if you believe it couldn't possibly be true. If you hear your child over-generalising, correcting him and telling him he is exaggerating, dreaming or imagining things may irritate him and he could shut down communication with you. As much as it can be tempting as a parent to give him a reality check, keep in mind that for him, in that moment, *it is true.*

Be a great help to your child by assisting him to see the reality of the situation for himself. A useful phrase I use in coaching is, *'So that is true for you…you believe no one will ever like you.'* It doesn't matter whether I agree with the statement or not, it's not about me!

If your child is over-generalising he may:
- Jump to conclusions – *'Four girls hate me so the rest of the girls must hate me too'*
- Take only a few facts or none at all, and jump to premature

conclusions and assume they are true – *'She didn't say hello to me so she must hate me too'*
- Assume a negative experience in one area pervades every aspect of his life – *'They hate me at school so they will hate me at basketball too'*
- Not notice the finer distinctions
- Not be able to see possible solutions

Have you checked for yourself if you over-generalise? Are there times when you jump to conclusions, and make assumptions based on a few facts or your past experiences? Most of us do this to a degree. The questions you might find helpful here are:
- What, if any assumptions, have I made about my child, my child being bullied, or my parenting skills?
- What, if any conclusions, have I jumped to without first checking in with my child?

If you ask yourself these questions and realise you have over-generalised, made assumptions, or jumped to conclusions, that's fantastic! Now that you're aware of it, you have the opportunity to check your facts and reach a new, different or more accurate awareness. You could also celebrate the fact you are not perfect and will make mistakes, and that's okay because it's part of the wonderful experience of being human!

If you discover your child is over-generalising, help him to explore and clarify his statements. Ask him to give detailed information about any vague terms or phrases he has used. Explore what your child means by his statement by asking the 'What…?', 'When…?', 'Where…?', 'Which…?', 'Who…?' and

'Why…?' questions. Remember, you are curious and interested, and coming from a neutral point of view. The slightest note of accusation or sarcasm in your voice risks the doors to communication with your child being slammed shut.

For example, let's say your child says, *'Everyone at school hates me'*. Curiously and respectfully, ask him some clarification questions:

- How do you know they hate you?
- Who specifically hates you?
- What do you mean by hate?
- Hates you in what way?
- When do they hate you?

Once your child has examined his belief, he can decide if he would like to continue to over-generalise or if he could think about his statement in a different way. It's up to your child to make this decision. Although you can't force him to change the way he thinks, you can hold up a mirror to him and let him know he doesn't have to think this way. You can let him know he has choices.

In general, avoid the question 'Why…?' when the statement is negative. If you ask, *'Why does everyone hate you?'* or *'Why do you believe everyone hates you?'*, your child will justify, find evidence and explain the reasons, as well as possibly go into a long story of *'he said, she said'*. To help your child, you don't need the long story! Use the 'Why…?' questions for when your child is speaking positively: *'Why would you want to choose to feel neutral about this?'* *'Why have you decided to be* Unbullyable?'

What is discounting?
We have explored whether your child is an all-or-nothing thinker, if he personalises things or over-generalises things. There is one

more common thinking style often present in children who experience bullying: discounting. Discounting and all-or-nothing thinking often go hand in hand. They are similar, but different. Discounting sounds like this: 'I'm not good at anything.'

Discounting is when we choose not to give things value. It's a way of devaluing. When we discount, we decide things don't have much value or meaning. We don't count them as important to us. When overdone, it's possible to discount things to the point where we become so blind to what we are discounting we don't even see them!

If your child is thinking in a 'discounting' style he may:
- Not value positives
- Believe what he does is never good enough
- Have trouble counting any positive things about himself
- See no pleasure in achieving the small steps of the journey: *'It's not completely finished so it's nothing'*
- Have difficulty building on what he has already achieved because it *'didn't count'*

A child who is in the habit of discounting might not notice positive interactions. He might not notice when other children are being kind to him or want to play with him. In the front of his mind are the bullying incidents. Positive playground or social experiences are pushed to the back of his mind because they don't 'count', and are not considered as important or significant.

If you take the time to listen carefully to your child, it's possible to discover if he's a discounting thinker or a counting thinker. You will hear him say, *'No one likes me.'* When you ask specific questions about who likes him, you may find there are other children in his school or class who do like him. But to your child they don't count, they don't matter: *'I don't have any friends. Well, I only have two friends but they don't count because they are in the other class.'*

Do you tend to discount, devalue, or not acknowledge or celebrate your successes along the way to achieving something? *'I was meant to do thirty minutes of exercise five days a week. I only did two days this week, so I might as well not bother. What is two days going to do? Nothing.'*

Or do you count? *'I planned to exercise each day this week and I did exercise two days. That's better than the week before!'*

As you think about and become aware of your own thinking in regard to parenting, what do you become aware of? Do you discount or devalue the job you are doing raising your child? Or do you value and celebrate and count progressions?

You can help your child to be his own biggest fan! Look for the positives, the smallest achievements, and no matter how tiny they are, point them out to your child. Invite him to celebrate his small achievements. To a child who does not want to go to school because of bullying, say, *'Wow! You got up and went to school three days this week!'*

Counting reinforces feelings and behaviours. As your child acknowledges and celebrates small successes, he begins to build up the thinking and feelings that go with those successful moments, and replicates them.

You can value and make significant anything your child does well. For example, if he tells you the bully tried to bully him five times, and four of those times he was upset and reacted by screaming at the bully but on one occasion he was able to choose to be unaffected, then tell him, *'Fantastic! You were able to choose how you felt that one time! Good on you!'* You are counting and valuing the one success, despite the four times he believed he was not able to choose how he felt or acted in response to the bullying.

By celebrating, encouraging and helping him to acknowledge his progress you are encouraging your child to:
- Take the credit for small achievements
- Notice the small steps he has made along the way
- Build on what he has already achieved
- See value in things, even if only to a small degree
- Understand the significance of each progression of the journey
- Reflect on his successes, no matter how small

Maree's story

When I discovered my seven-year-old son was being bullied I felt like a failure as a parent. It was as if all my years of effort and time I put into building up his self-esteem was wiped out from underneath me. Gone. I was raising this child as a single parent, teaching him right from wrong, and to be a fair and gentle person.

Through coaching I discovered my discounting pattern was a way of thinking I had applied to myself my whole life. I discounted many things about myself. The strange thing is, with my son I 'counted' every step – I would comment and celebrate all his achievements, no matter how small. That's why I was shocked when he told me he was being bullied.

Looking back now I realise I didn't cope well with the news because I was making it about me and my parenting. I began discounting my parenting, the very thing I thought I was doing well at. Once I became aware of the fact I hadn't 'failed' him as a parent, I was once again able to value my role in him becoming who he is. Now I 'count' the contribution I make. But in the beginning, it vanished – I discounted it.

Your child's thinking styles are a unique combination of a number of things. Imagine how a child who personalises everything (all or nothing) and, in addition, discounts, experiences bullying attempts *in a different way* from a child who makes the bullying about the bully and not about himself (does not personalise), who thinks in degrees ('they don't try to bully me every day') and who counts progress, even the slightest progress?

Your child's thinking styles have an influence on how he experiences other people's attempts to bully him. With awareness and support, your child can change his thinking styles to those that are more resourceful, and move himself towards becoming *Unbullyable*.

Chapter summary

- Knowing how your child re-presents things in his mind will assist you to understand and communicate with him.
- Some people are highly visual and see images and pictures, others use sounds and produce soundtracks, while others process information by noticing how they feel about it.
- We use a mixture of all three ways of processing and representing information; most of us have a favourite.
- The four most common thinking styles I see in children affected by bullying are, all-or-nothing thinking, personalising, over-generalising and discounting.
- If we perceive bullying as a threat to our personal safety, our brains kick into survival mode and we experience a 'fight or flight' response.
- Sometimes all-or-nothing thinking is very useful, and at other times unresourceful or limiting.
- Personalising is another thinking style common among bullied children. If your child personalises, he takes what

someone says or does and makes it about him, even when it's not.
- Over-generalising is when we jump to conclusions and make assumptions based on a few facts.
- Discounting is when we choose not to give things value. It's a way of devaluing. When we discount, we decide things don't have much value or meaning.

Moving forward

Whoo hoo! We have finished the chapters that offer you the tools, strategies and techniques for helping your child choose to be unaffected by other people's attempts to bully him. By now the pieces of the *Unbullyable* puzzle are fitting into place. I encourage you to take all that information and apply it to cyberbullying.

12

Cyberbullying

There is no need to spend time bombarding you with the most recent statistics on cyberbullying. There are *hundreds* of research studies conducted to explore the prevalence of cyberbullying among children worldwide. You can easily find them on the internet (How ironic!). In a nutshell, the statistics regarding the number of children reporting they are being cyberbullied are frightening.

If your child is using social media, her chance of experiencing some form of cyberbullying is high. Most parents are not interested in detailed statistics, *they just want to know how to help*. While cyberbullying is a variation of bullying using new and different tools, be assured you can support your child in the same way as you would for any form of bullying.

In this chapter we bring together the *Unbullyable* approach to bullying and apply it to cyberbullying. We explore:
- What is cyberbullying?
- How does cyberbullying differ from other types of bullying?
- What do you believe about cyberbullying?
- What do children believe about cyberbullying?
- What is the language of cyberbullying?

- How can you keep your child safe online?
- How can you help your child?

What is cyberbullying?

Cyberbullying occurs when children use technology such as text messages, emails and the internet (Facebook, Twitter, YouTube or other social media) to bully others. The bully usually posts comments about the target, or photos of the target with the intention of causing the target harm. The term 'cyberbullying' is used when talking about bullying between children. When an adult is harassing children or teenagers, this is known as 'cyber harassment' or 'cyber stalking'. In this chapter, we explore cyberbullying.

The Australian Communications and Media Authority describes cyberbullying in this way:[29]

> *Cyberbullying occurs when the internet, e-mail or mobile phones are used to deliberately and repeatedly engage in hostile behaviour to harm someone. Cyberbullying can include harassment or behaviour that threatens, humiliates or intimidates someone, such as sending abusive texts or e-mails, excluding others from online chats or communication or posting unkind messages or inappropriate images on social networking sites.*

From an *Unbullyable* perspective, for a child to be successfully cyberbullied, the following needs to occur:

- The target believes the bully's intention of the words, comments, posts or photo etc. is to cause her harm
- The target believes the bully's posts have the power to 'make' her feel worthless, angry, hurt, or like nothing

- The target experiences an unresourceful state when viewing the posts/comments
- The target believes she can be cyberbullied
- The bully's words, comments, posts are repeatedly directed at the target, or are specifically about the target.

Like any other form of bullying, your child has the power to interrupt, disrupt and stubbornly refuse to be affected by the cyberbullying attempt. For a child to be unaffected by another child's attempt to bully her, the following needs to occur:
- The target believes the bully's intention of the words, comments and posts *cannot* cause her harm. She knows the words, comments or posts belong to the bully, and are not about her, rather about the bully
- The target believes the bully's posts *cannot* 'make' her feel anything. She knows she chooses how she thinks and feels about the bully's attempt to cyberbully her
- The target remains in a *resourceful* state when viewing the posts, knowing she chooses the meaning she gives to the posts. She knows she can step into an *Unbullyable* state at any time she chooses
- The target believes she *can't* be cyberbullied. She knows that while someone may *try* to cyberbully her, she doesn't have to be affected by that person's attempts

How does cyberbullying differ from other types of bullying?

Cyberbullying has certain characteristics that make it a unique form of bullying. A bully can attempt to cyberbully the target twenty-four hours a day, seven days a week. The bullying attempts are continuous; they occur during school hours, after school, at night, on weekends and school holidays. In addition, some cyberbullying occurs anonymously, with the bully hiding behind a shield of anonymity. In many cases the bullying behaviour is increasingly hurtful and aggressive because it is easier to deliver when it's not face to face. As one child shared with me, *'Behind the screen, they're more mean'*.

While cyberbullies choose to be aggressive and say or write things they wouldn't say face to face, cyberbullying is also immediate. Within one lunchtime, the information can be spread across most schools in your town. Once in Cyberland, information is impossible to delete or contain. A photo, comment or rumour about your child can go 'viral'. Yes, it might seem scary and overwhelming at first, but remember, your child can choose the way she thinks about it. Like any other form of bullying, for cyberbullying to be effective, the target has to believe the post, comment, or photo can *make* her feel sad, upset, annoyed, like a failure, or a loser.

> *The effectiveness of the cyberbullying behaviour displayed by the bully is determined by the meaning the target gives the behaviour.*

For example, the effectiveness of the comment on Facebook is determined by the meaning your child gives to the comment. How your child chooses to feel, and what she thinks, says and does in response to the comment, is determined by her. Of course it is normal and understandable for your child to feel upset, angry or disappointed when someone says or writes something nasty about her on Facebook, but you can support your child to choose what she would like to do with those emotions. Support your child by listening to understand her, and not to judge or punish her.

What do you believe about cyberbullying?

Cyberbullying is one type of bullying that receives a great deal of publicity because it's a relatively new phenomenon. Parents can have a 'fear' reaction to the phrase 'cyberbullying' simply because it's new, unfamiliar and an unknown. Your beliefs about cyberbullying affect how your child communicates to you about her experience.

Consider how you think *about* cyberbullying. Do you have a physical reaction to the phrase 'cyberbullying'? Some parents literally hold their breath when they hear the term. They freeze with fear. One cyber safety expert I listened to described cyberbullying *as 'bullying on steroids'*. It's no wonder many parents are fearful!

The great news is that you can reduce your anxiety – there's no need to panic! If you believe, *'I don't know anything about Facebook or how it works – I don't know how to help',* be reassured you can help your child without having a PhD in information technology. What if you could think about cyberbullying as simply one form of bullying? The 'cyber' part is the new term used to describe the way in which the bullying is delivered. The word 'cyber' might not have been around when you were growing up, but it's just a word! It's a word to describe a type of bullying, like exclusion, physical, verbal and *cyber*. As always, the first step in helping your child is to discover and understand what she believes about cyberbullying.

What do children believe about cyberbullying?

Remember the concept that beliefs hold behaviour in place we explored in Chapter Three? Beliefs hold behaviour in place, so in order to change behaviour, we need to explore beliefs. Your child's beliefs about cyberbullying, the internet and social media in general hold her behaviour in place. Telling your child to change her online behaviour without understanding what she believes will not result in change. Understanding what drives and motivates your child to use the internet – to have a Facebook account, for example – enables you to help and support her.

Most children use the internet as a way of staying connected to their peer group. They gain a sense of belonging from using it. Using social media keeps them up to date with what's happening, and they remain in the loop and don't miss information vitally important to them (even if it seems trivial to us!). For some children it is a status symbol to have the latest technology, and deleting their Facebook account is simply not an option they would consider.

Discover your child's beliefs about cyberbullying by asking her directly, 'Do you believe you can be cyberbullied?' If you're not sure how to do this, use the information in Chapter Five to have a conversation to find out what your child believes. In Chapter Five we explored how to be in rapport with your child, listen without judgement, and get yourself out of the way to listen, truly listen. Use that information to ask your child the following questions:

- What do you believe about cyberbullying?
- How would you know if someone was trying to cyberbully you?
- What do your friends believe about cyberbullying?
- Can you be cyberbullied? If so, how?

- Has anyone tried to bully you on the internet or by text messages?
- If you believed someone was trying to cyberbully you, how would you choose to respond?

As your child answers your questions, listen for her experience and her language. Then check in with yourself. What, if anything, are you *assuming* about your child's beliefs and experience of cyberbullying? Is it possible for you to put your own beliefs about cyberbullying aside and understand what it is like for her based on her map of the world? If you feel it's useful for your child, explore what it *means* to her to be online.

Find out what is important to your child about having a Facebook or Twitter account. Is it about her identity – how she sees herself and how she would like other people to see her? What would *not* being on Facebook mean to your child? Is it not being part of the group? Is it about a sense of belonging? What else does it mean to your child?

In Chapter Six we explored self-esteem. Use questions to discover if your child's self-esteem is conditional upon how many 'friends' she has on Facebook. I have coached teenagers with over one thousand Facebook friends. How many friends does your child have on Facebook? Does your child have a relationship with these 'friends'? What motivates your child to have the amount of 'friends' she does?

Jess, aged nine, (yes, too young for Facebook!) shared: *'The more friends I have on Facebook the more popular I am. It means people like me.'* And Samuel, aged eleven: *'I don't have many friends at school, but I have twenty-two friends on Facebook. Some of my Facebook friends never talk to me at school – and that's okay.'*

When having this conversation with your child, keep in mind that she may have already had a cyberbullying experience and not told you at the time. When I ask children why they don't tell their parents about being cyberbullied, the number one response is fear their phone or internet access will be restricted or taken away from them. While this might seem like a great negotiating tool for some parents, the internet is the way of life for many children. It makes sense to them to protect and fight for it. They fear that, *'If I tell Mum or Dad about the cyberbullying, I will lose access to the internet'*.

Many parents ask their child, *'Why do you even read it?'* The biggest reason children who are cyberbullied continue reading Facebook posts is they *want to know* what is being written about them. They want to be informed. They want to know (if possible) who posted the cyberbullying attempts, and if anyone 'liked', shared or commented on the posts. Who, if anyone, defended them? They value the option of replying or defending themselves, even if they choose not to.

What is the language of cyberbullying?

'I hate the term cyberbullying. *It's such a babyish way to describe what goes on.'*

Cam, aged seventeen.

As explained in Chapter Five, it's important to use the language your child uses when talking about the internet. For example, my teenage daughter informs me that only 'old' people refer to Facebook as *'the* Facebook'! Matching your child's language is valuable in gaining rapport and understanding your child's world. Be aware the language is changing at a rapid rate. Give yourself permission to not know what words and phrases mean. Phrases that are current now will be out of date and even obsolete in a relatively short time period: 'like', 'share', 'comment', 'tagging', 'hash tag', 'friending' etc.

The following statements are examples of how children describe their cyberbullying experience:
- Posting for me to go and kill myself – asking me how I'm going to do it
- Setting up harmful sites on social media such as 'hate sites' about me
- Spreading rumours about me, like I'm gay
- Threatening me (with acts of violence, or death)
- Warning me to watch my back, they are going to bash me
- Posting embarrassing photos of me on Facebook etc.
- Cutting me out of group photos on Facebook etc.
- Hacking into my Facebook account and writing stuff about me or other people

Your child may also have her own language among her peers, as Carissa's statement demonstrates: '*…I thought we were friends, and then she small dotted me! I couldn't believe she did that.*' I had no idea what being 'small dotted' meant to Carissa, so I respectfully and curiously asked her to explain it. She stated a small dot at the end of the 'chat' on Facebook is a not very nice way of saying, 'I'm ending this conversation NOW'. It's like hanging up on someone on the phone.

The meaning and power Carissa and her friends give to a small dot sounded significant, so I asked her to clarify. Carissa and her friends *never* put a small dot at the end of their sentences. When her friend 'small dotted' her, it was a big deal. It held high meaning and importance to Carissa and her online friends. For other people Carissa's age, a small dot is just a full stop used for finishing a sentence. It's the meaning your child gives something, like a dot, a comment, a photo and so on that's important to know to understand the situation. It's useful to ask your child what something means to them.

How can you keep your child safe online?

Cyber safety generally refers to being safe online. Its focus is on keeping children safe from bullies, paedophiles and con artists, or anyone who has an intention to harm children through the internet. There are many cyber safety programs aimed at helping children and parents identify the risks children face online. Cyber safety programs focus on educating children and their parents about the risks, and putting strategies in place to minimise and manage them. For the latest information, I suggest you do your own internet search. You will find plenty of information and resources for children and parents.

While cyber safety is important, most cyber safety resources do not specifically address cyberbullying. The ones that do include cyberbullying address it at the behaviour level only, and most often ignore the thinking and beliefs of the children. I encourage you to combine both: assist your child to be cyber safe in her behaviour and *Unbullyable* in her thinking.

> *It's the meaning your child gives something that is most important.*

You can encourage your child to be safe online by establishing boundaries and safeguards. For example, at what age (if ever) will you allow your child to open a Facebook account? Legally, children under thirteen years of age cannot open a Facebook account. But there have been reported cases of children as young as five years old with Facebook accounts. If you allow your child to open a Facebook or Twitter account etc., then consider how you monitor her involvement in cyberland. For example, talk with her about limiting who knows her password. If your child has a Facebook account, ensure you learn the basics yourself and 'friend' her. Monitor what she is posting and how much time she spends interacting with other Facebook users.

My teenage daughter does not have her own Facebook or Twitter account. She 'reads' my Facebook account and her friends'. She's online in other ways – for example, Instagram and YouTube – so potentially she may be exposed to something she finds disturbing. If this occurs, we could use it as a learning opportunity for her to experience dealing with a tough situation. If she really wants her own account I would consider it knowing my decision is based on *my map of the world* and *my beliefs*, and is influenced by *my experience* of seeing first-hand how cyberbullying can affect children. Your decision too is based on your map of the world, your experiences and your beliefs.

As much as some parents want to protect their child from images or posts that are violent, pornographic or disturbing in some way, it's not always possible. Trying to completely protect your child is difficult, and most children *want to be online*. As Facebook and other online social media sites change and evolve, there are many ways in which your child will try to outsmart you.

What motivates them? For older children, they want their privacy. Just like you wouldn't want them listening into your phone calls, they want their space too. It's not that they are doing anything wrong; they just don't need *their parents listening in*! It's a fine line between monitoring their access and online activity, and sending them underground. Limiting your child's use of social media is tricky. If you establish a situation where you are trying to outsmart your child, you will probably lose! Remember, your child has a whole network of friends who can answer her techno questions, and they are *highly motivated* to figure out how to outsmart their parents!

Kylie's story

> *My two teenage children had mobile phones and were on Facebook all the time. They had their mobile phones at school, connected to the internet in the classroom, so they were on Facebook during school hours. I was horrified the day my daughter boasted that she could 'look' as if she was writing with her right hand, but actually be texting with her left hand while her mobile phone was in her school uniform pocket!*
>
> *I discovered both my son and daughter were on Facebook in their bed sometimes until one or two in the morning. It was out of control. I took action by demanding they leave their mobile phones charging on the kitchen bench every night. As I went to bed I'd check the phones were on the bench. I thought it was working well. I thought I was so smart! About three months later I found out they had been taking their SIM cards*

out and sharing an old spare mobile phone so they could be Facebooking at night.

I realised they are one step ahead of me. I reluctantly opened a Facebook account and made them 'friend' me. Now I've heard they block me from reading certain posts, so I'm not sure if that is working either. I'm hoping they don't remember they also 'friended' my very cool sister-in-law. We have an agreement that if she reads anything that I should be concerned about, she will let me know. That's reassuring.

How can you help your child?

There are many websites available with information for parents on how to help their child if they are being cyberbullied. Some use plain English to explain social media to parents who may not use it themselves. In addition to your own research, many schools and communities offer 'Cyber Safety' information nights for parents. If your child's school has not organised one of these, request that they do.

You can help your child to respond to cyberbullying attempts in the same way as other forms of bullying. Just because cyberbullying wasn't around when you were growing up, doesn't mean you can't help your child. You can, even if you don't know the first thing about Facebook. Your limiting beliefs *about* cyberbullying, and not being Facebook savvy, would be the only things stopping you from helping your child.

Use the *Unbullyable* approach outlined in this book and apply it to cyberbullying. Above all other things, your child wants love and support. If your child has shared with you that she is being cyberbullied, she is most likely seeking love, understanding, comfort and reassurance.

Chapter summary

- If your child is using social media, her chance of experiencing some form of cyberbullying is high.
- Cyberbullying occurs when children use technology such as text messages, emails and the internet (Facebook, Twitter, YouTube or other social media) to bully others.
- The term 'cyberbullying' is used when talking about bullying between children. When an adult is harassing children or teenagers, this is known as 'cyber harassment' or 'cyber stalking'.
- Cyberbullying has certain characteristics that make it unique to other forms of bullying. It can be constant 24/7, anonymous and immediate.
- The effectiveness of the bullying behaviour displayed by the bully is determined by the meaning the target gives the behaviour.
- Your beliefs about cyberbullying affect how your child communicates to you about her experience.
- Your child's beliefs about cyberbullying and the internet and so on hold her behaviour in place. Telling your child to change her online behaviour without understanding what she believes will not result in change.
- Many children who are cyberbullied continue reading Facebook posts as they *want to know* what is being written about them.
- Matching your child's language is valuable in gaining rapport with her and understanding her world.
- Cyber safety generally refers to being safe online. Its focus is on keeping children safe from bullies, paedophiles and

con artists, or anyone who has an intention to harm children through the internet.
- While cyber safety is important, most cyber safety resources do not specifically address cyberbullying.
- Assist your child to be cyber safe in her behaviour, and *Unbullyable* in her thinking.
- There are many websites available with information for parents on how to help their child if they are being cyberbullied.

Moving forward

Are you ready to put the last piece of the puzzle into place? The final chapter explores the children doing the bullying – the bullies. I offer you a fascinating insight into their beliefs, esteem, power, states and thinking styles.

How is it possible that bullying your child makes sense to them? That's what we explore in the next chapter.

13

Bullies

In this chapter we explore a topic that always raises much discussion when I introduce it at training sessions or presentations – bullies. People seem fascinated with understanding why children bully. It's an interesting and complex topic.

To fully understand the bullying experience, it's useful to consider the beliefs of the child doing the bullying. Some parents react defensively when exploring this topic, so I will clarify right from the start: *I am not defending or justifying a child who bullies another child.* I believe understanding why children bully can help you to support your child. It's like being familiar with all the pieces of the puzzle so you can see the solution.

In this chapter we explore:
- Why do children bully?
- How do bullies select their targets?
- What are some characteristics common to bullies?
- Are there different types of bullies?
- How can bullies transform themselves?

I've been privileged enough to coach children who bully and, by using a non-judgemental approach, without analysing, I can act as a mirror for them. When I respectfully hold up a mirror, children 'see' themselves as others see them, possibly for the first time. They see what has been, up until then, blind to them.

To hold up a mirror to children who bully is an interesting experience. Sometimes they don't like what they see, and are motivated to change. Other times, they respond with a 'What?' because they see their behaviour as normal – they don't see a problem. For these children, their thinking and bullying behaviour makes perfect sense to them, given their map of the world.

To remain non-judgemental when coaching bullies I consider every child precious, valuable and know they are more than their behaviours. I imagine the possibilities within them. I see their goodness and their potential – even if they don't. Yes - *even* the teenage boy I recently coached who bashed his classmate to the point of hospitalisation. His behaviour made sense to him at the time. Don't get me wrong, his choice to bash his classmate was disgraceful and he needs to be held accountable for his behaviour, yet I know he is more than his behaviours. My job is to coach him so *he* can know he is more than his behaviours. My job is to help *him* see the goodness and potential within him so he can choose to not bully anymore.

Through coaching bullies I have insights into bullies' thinking styles and beliefs. They are children who make poor decisions based on their understanding of the world. To them, there is a reason to bully. I appreciate this may be hard to accept when *your* child is the target of the bullying behaviour. Understanding the reasons another child bullies your child may not make it any less painful for you and your child, but I believe the bully is also in pain. I'm yet to coach a happy, confident bully who actually likes who they are. I have found common thinking among bullies include a lack of personal power, negative self-image, poor communication skills and general unhappiness.

I am reluctant to even label a child as a 'bully'. In an ideal world, I would refer to a bully as 'a child who at times engages in bullying behaviour'. It sounds over-the-top-politically-correct I know, and it would be a bit awkward within this book, so I use the term 'bully' instead. Most children I coach start off hating the child who is bullying them, however it is very common, even in young children, that by the end of the coaching program the children do not hate the bully anymore. Instead, they develop empathy for them as they compare their future to a bully's. They often develop an understanding and compassion beyond their years.

Why do children bully?

How is it possible bullying behaviour *makes sense* to a child? Generally, children bully to fulfil a need. There is a positive intention or a secondary gain driving their behaviour. They get *something* out of it. As we explored in Chapter Seven, a bully may be unable to gain a sense of personal power from within, they bully others to feel powerful, only the powerful feeling does not last, so they have to bully again. This is why bullies will often attack and withdraw, then attack and withdraw. This theory makes logical sense, but bullying is not always logical. Here are some other reasons children have shared:

- *School is boring so I bully because there is nothing else to do*
- *It's just what me and my mates do*
- *She deserves it*
- *It's just mucking around*
- *If I don't join in they might bully me instead*

- *He said if I don't bully I can't hang around with him and he would bash me*
- *It's fun*
- *I don't know*

Some bullies are bored at school, they bully as a form of entertainment. As one bully explained:

We go at him in class until he cracks it. It's kind of like a game to see how long it takes for him to go off. And it's fun to come up with different ways to get to him. It's hilarious when he goes off and chucks a spaz. We laugh so much.

Sadly, the target is not laughing, and does not think it is hilarious.

Some bullies try to justify their bullying behaviour by blaming the target or stating the target deserves it: '*He's a little pain in the arse. He's full of himself. He's really annoying so we beat him up.*' Then there are other, more complex reasons. As Clinton, aged fifteen, shared:

I don't know how to get along with kids my own age. They are stupid and make me angry. I hate a lot of them. I don't know how to talk to them. I hang out with adults at home. It's like I want to be part of them but I'm different to them. I don't fit in.

I asked Clinton, 'What's it like in that very moment when you're bullying? What's it like for you?'

'Lonely. Sad and lonely'.

I was surprised to hear Clinton say he was lonely and sad when bullying. In coaching he had portrayed himself as bigger, tougher and smarter than his peers, yet when he explored his experience of bullying, he was lonely and sad.

And thirteen-year-old Heidi also surprised me with her reasoning:

> *I bully and bully and then I fight them. At my school, punch-ons are a big deal. When there's a punch-on, everyone comes running and stands around me and cheers and watches me. They yell out my name, 'Heidi, Heidi, go Heidi. Smash her.' I like that they yell out my name.*

When I asked her the same question as I asked Clinton, what was it like for her, she answered, *'Comfort. It's like comfort.'*

To Heidi, bullying gave her comfort. She explained how it made sense to her, and described a childhood of abuse and abandonment. In coaching she explored other ways of seeking comfort that did not involve bullying. She now believes 'punch-ons are stupid' and won't fight anymore, even when asked to by her peers: *'I have nothing to prove. They are scared of me because they know I can fight, so now I don't have to fight anymore. It's better.'*

It may be that you will never know the reason why another child is trying to bully your child. We can assume bullying is fulfilling a need for the bully, and has nothing to do with your child. This means bullying is always about the bully, and not the target. Your child may be the target right now, but the bully could have easily chosen another child to bully. Once your child moves from bullied to *Unbullyable*, the bully will most likely move on to the next target. Interestingly, most children can guess who the next target will be. How do they know that? How do bullies know who to pick on? To find out I asked the people who know best – the bullies.

How do bullies select their targets?

To make their bullying attempts successful, bullies select children who they judge are bullyable. Bullies have shared with me that they look for children who *look like they can be bullied.* They select their targets strategically.

They use information such as a child's posture, body language, voice, eye cues and their social connectedness within the school to guess how bullyable a child is. Then they test out their selection. Leigh, age thirteen, explained how he selected his potential targets:

> *At the start of Year Seven I looked around for the scared, weird kids who were on their own. The way they stood and talked and looked told me straight away if I could bully them or not. Then I tested them out. I would say something smart to them to see how they handled me. The kids who backed down straight away were the ones I went after. The ones who said stuff back to me were a maybe, depending on how they said it and if they had any mates or not. I looked for the weird kids with no mates who just kind of shrivelled up when I tested them out.*

Bullies might look for a specific reason to target another child. If there is anything different about a child, that difference could be used as a reason (in the mind of the bully) to bully them. For example, if a child is from a different background, is fat, skinny, tall, short, looks different in any way, acts different in any way, is considered too smart, too stupid, eats tuna for lunch, likes certain music, doesn't like certain music, has body odour, bad breath, is missing a limb, sings, has pimples, wears braces, wears glasses, has freckles, wears the wrong shoes, has the wrong phone, has a funny surname, is physically under-developed, is an early developer, likes to read, can't read...you get the idea! There is no logic here because the bullying is about the bully, not the target.

> *If there is no obvious reason to bully a child (according to the bully), the bully will make one up!*

What are some characteristics common to bullies?

If you were to undertake your own internet research on bullies, here are examples of what you are likely to find:[30]

- Bullies lack empathy
- Bullies lack power, they try to bully others to make them feel powerful
- Bullies become less popular as they get older. They may seem cool now, but it won't last
- Children who bully are more likely to end up with a criminal record as an adult than those who don't bully
- Children who bully are more likely to behave violently as an adult than those who don't bully
- Children who bully are more likely to experience relationship problems as an adult than those who don't bully

In my experience in coaching children who bully, I have noticed some similarities among them. Bullies:
- are disempowered, they express little belief in their sense of personal powers
- feel like they are different or separate from other children
- often lack social and communication skills

- are often also being bullied, either at school or within their own family
- often do not like themselves or their behaviour.

Are there different types of bullies?

Just as all targets of bullying are not the same, bullies also differ. I believe there are two main 'types' of bullies: children who know they bully, and children who have no idea how they affect the people around them.

1. Children who know they bully

Some children know they bully others and identify themselves as a 'bully'. Once they are given and have accepted the label, they often don't know how to free themselves of it, even if they want to.

Tilly, aged twelve, considered herself a bully and wanted to shake the label. Here are some of her thoughts:

> *I am a bully. I have been since Grade Three. I want to stop. I want to stop making people see I am a bad person. I want to treat people better than I am now. I don't have any friends. I want some. I accept the fact no one wants to be my friend. People don't really like me. I want to change; I am over the way I am. I just want to be a normal twelve-year-old kid and not have attitude. I want to show people who I really am but it's hard for me. I'm hidden under the bullying. They are afraid of me.*

I was blown away when Tilly shared those thoughts with me. She identified with being a bully, yet didn't want to be one. She was aware of how others experienced her, and wanted to change their perception of her. I worked with Tilly for a few months, and by the end of our time together she had made one friend. For Tilly, this was a huge achievement. She was so excited to have a friend. It meant so much to her that *one student* liked her. That one friendship had a huge impact on how she saw herself as a person. The possibility of having more friends was opening up for her.

Unlike Tilly, who identified with being a bully and wanted to change, there are children who identify themselves as a bully and don't want to change. They see no reason to change their behaviour, because it makes sense to them and they are getting something out of it. In some situations these children bully and *get away with it*. No one holds them accountable for their behaviour. They are seemingly untouchable.

As a parent explained:

When I told the school Billie Jo was the girl bullying my daughter the principal and vice principal refused to believe me. Billie Jo was the school captain! They refused to believe Billie Jo could be a bully. They suggested my daughter was jealous of Billie Jo, or wanting attention. They basically called my daughter a liar.

A teacher shared his experience of working at a private school:

This kid was untouchable. He was the footy star at a school where footy is everything. He was god and he knew it. He was smart, rich, popular, good-looking; the girls loved him, the other teachers loved him. For eighteen months he and his mates bullied me. He knew that I knew there was no way the school would kick him out. The school needed him. He made my life hell some days.

And a mum whose son attended a school focused on academic achievement:

> *The girl bullying my son was a high academic achiever. She was the type of student the school wanted to hang onto. Academic achievement is the main priority. I mean this school asks students who were not performing academically to leave in fear they might bring the school's academic rating down. When we reported the bullying, the school suggested I pull my son out of the school and move him to a different school. I couldn't believe it. My son was gutted.*

2. Children who are unaware other people experience them as a bully

Is it possible children cannot know that others think of them as a bully? I wouldn't have thought so until I met some of these children.

I believe a small percentage of children have *no idea* others consider them a bully. And they certainly don't see themselves as a bully. They lack self-awareness. To them, and according to their map of the world, their bullying behaviour is normal. I coached a boy who told me he punched other children to get what he wanted because that's what happened at home. Using threats and physically harming others was, sadly, normal behaviour to him.

Some bullies are genuinely unaware of how other people experience them. They are often focused on themselves, their own survival and safety, and what they can get from other people to fulfil their needs. They lack the ability to see through the eyes of others. It's common for them to also lack basic communication and social skills. So yes, I believe a child can be a bully and not have the self-awareness to know it. For Linda, discovering that came as a shock to her.

Linda's story

I was bullied by a girl at my school. She made my life hell at high school. She was a bully and I was terrified of her. I'm now in my thirties and two years ago I connected with some high school friends on Facebook. Through friends of friends on Facebook she sent me a friend request. I was disgusted. How dare she act as if nothing had happened? I thought about it for a few days and then I accepted her friend request so I could check her out. Turned out she lives in the next suburb.

She messaged me asking if I wanted to meet up for coffee. I didn't know what to do. I considered it for a few months before I accepted as I had some things I wanted to say to her! I wanted her to know that despite her bullying I turned out okay. And I wanted an apology. I was nervous when I met with her and told her how she had made me feel, how she had treated me and how she had affected me. She listened and told me she didn't ever remember bullying me. We both cried. She said she had lots of problems at home during high school. Turns out she doesn't work, has not had a family and has bipolar disorder. It's bizarre, I know, but we are now friends. I've been a great support for her in the past six months. I didn't get the apology I was searching for; I gained a friend.

How can bullies transform themselves?

We can support children to choose not to bully anymore. While I believe we definitely should hold bullies accountable for their bullying behaviour, punishing the behaviour alone does not stop them from bullying in the future. Telling a child to 'stop bullying' doesn't work, because addressing bullying at the behavioural level and not the belief level is ineffective. Their beliefs hold the behaviour in place, and punishing the behaviour of the bullies does not change their beliefs.

Part of the solution to reducing bullying *is to hold the bullies accountable for their behaviour and, at the same time, encourage them to empower themselves so they don't have to bully anymore.* Plus, we need to hold bullies accountable for their attempted bullying. This means holding bullies accountable for their behaviour even when their bullying attempts fail because their targets choose to be unaffected by the attempt.

The solution is to empower bullies until they gain their sense of personal power from within themselves; they don't have to intimidate others to feel powerful. When coaching children who bully I curiously explore:

- Is it safe for you to not bully?
- What would you be doing instead of bullying?
- Do you have permission to not bully?
- What is the value in bullying?
- What, if anything, are you getting out of bullying?
- What is bullying costing you?

I also ask about the children's sense of personal power, their beliefs about others, the world, themselves etc. I have found most children who bully are disempowered, are lonely and don't know how to 'be' differently in the world. I ask them, 'Who is the you who, instead of bullying, treats people with kindness, respect and compassion?' I am excited when bullies realise they have a choice. The penny drops for them that they don't *have to bully*. They can choose to be different, once they *know* they have a choice.

Consider this statement from a child who bullies: *'I don't know how to not be a bully anymore. I want to stop, but I'm not sure how to.'* As I think about this child, I am optimistic about the future. As more adults understand the bullying experience, and how to encourage children to be *Unbullyable*, more can also support children who want to stop bullying. We can teach our children to become *Unbullyable*, and how to be empowered to choose who they are, and how they treat others. In addition to this, we can teach children how to *not bully in the first place*, or how to *stop bullying*, and choose again.

Imagine when children, parents and teachers support and encourage a child who bullies to change. I believe we can. With the information offered in this book, I believe it is possible for parents to support children to move from bullied to *Unbullyable*, and support children to move from 'bully' to empowered children who choose not to bully.

Chapter summary
- To fully understand the bullying experience, it's useful to consider the beliefs of the child doing the bullying.
- Understanding why children bully can help you to support your child.
- Bullies are children who make poor decisions based on their understanding of the world.
- Common thinking styles among bullies include a lack of personal power, a negative self-image, poor communication skills and general unhappiness.
- Children bully to fulfil a need. They get *something* out of it.
- Bullying is not always logical.

- Some bullies try to justify their bullying behaviour by blaming the target or stating the target deserves it.
- Bullying is always about the bully and not the target.
- To make their bullying attempts successful, bullies select children who they judge are bullyable.
- Bullies look for children who *look like they can be bullied*.
- Bullies use information such as a child's posture, body language, voice, eye cues and their social connectedness within the school to guess how bullyable a child is.
- If there is no obvious reason to bully a child, the bully will make one up.
- Bullies are often disempowered, feel like they are different or separate from other children, lack social and communication skills, and do not like themselves or their behaviour.
- Part of the solution to bullying is to hold bullies accountable for their behaviour, regardless of how it is received by the target.
- There are two main 'types' of bullies: children who know they bully, and children who have no idea how they affect the people around them.
- Punishing the behaviour of bullies does not change their beliefs. Part of the solution to bullying *is to help bullies empower themselves so they don't have to bully anymore.*
- As more adults understand the bullying experience, and how to encourage children to be *Unbullyable*, more can also support children who want to stop bullying.
- We can teach our children to become *Unbullyable*, and how to be empowered to choose who they are and how they treat others.

- We can teach children how to *not bully in the first place*, or how to *stop bullying* and choose again.

Moving forward

So while others may *try* to bully your child, you can encourage and support your child to choose to be *Unbullyable*. Imagine a world where everyone chooses to be *Unbullyable* – a world where each of us stubbornly refuses to allow other people's attempts to bully us be successful. If we all did that there would be no one left for bullies to bully! Imagine a future where bullies are held accountable for their behaviour and discover they don't need to try to bully others; instead, they focus their energy on *connecting* with others. I don't know about you, but this is the future I want for my children.

Afterword

You may doubt my vision or call me a dreamer (I don't mind because I am *Unbullyable*). I have been criticised for speaking up publically in a positive and optimistic way. The critics are those who cannot allow their thinking to expand beyond the current reality. They have trouble even *imagining* that we can do something about bullying. One influential person warned me to *'not get people's hopes up'*! I don't know about you, but I'm over the doom-and-gloom approach to addressing bullying. I've had enough of the current bullying affecting our precious children. I am hopeful we can make a difference. And when it comes to bullying, I'd rather be hopeful than hopeless.

Imagine yourself being part of this solution as you take the information from this book and apply, experiment and try on these skills. Discover for yourself what opens up for you and your children. What if the dictionaries of the future contained the word *'Unbullyable'* and the phrase 'attempted bullying'? Together, we can make a generational change that starts now. If you show your children how to be *Unbullyable*, they will raise their own *Unbullyable* children (your gorgeous grandchildren), and so on. Sounds good, doesn't it?

Will you join me on my mission to help ONE MILLION people of any age, from any nation, to choose to be *Unbullyable*? If you, your children, your family or friends would like to stand up and be counted as part of the *Unbullyable Million,* please visit my website and sign up to show your support. I know it's not going to happen overnight – I don't mind if it takes years! I encourage you to visit often and see how we are progressing. You will also find information and news about how together we can spread the *Unbullyable* message to our schools, local communities, politicians and the international stage. *Here's to our Unbullyable future generations!*

www.unbullyable.com.au

Resources and websites

Unbullyable App
Visit our website www.unbullyable.com.au for the latest news and developments including our *Unbullyable* App for your child's mobile phone.

Workshops
Sue Anderson is available to conduct her *Unbullyable* workshops for children, parents, teachers, organisations and workplaces. For more information on trainings and workshops please visit our website www.unbullyable.com.au or e-mail us at info@unbullyable.com.au

Coaching
If you or your child would like to experience one-on-one coaching with Sue Anderson, or any of our qualified *Unbullyable* coaches, contact us directly at www.unbullyable.com.au or www.good2gr8.com.au or email us at info@unbullyable.com.au

Presentations
If you believe your school, community group or workplace would be interested in an *Unbullyable* presentation, please contact us directly at www.unbullyable.com.au or email us at info@unbullyable.com.au

Anti-Bullying Organisations (Not-for-profit)
If you would like to contact or support anti-bullying organisations, Angel's Goal and Brodie's Law Foundation

are working proactively to spread the anti-bully message. Sue Anderson supports these two organisations and highly recommends you visit their websites to find out more.

Angel's Goal

www.angelsgoal.org.au

Brodie's Law Foundation

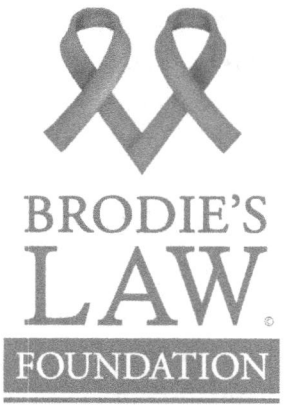

www.brodieslaw.org

Notes

1. Professor Donna Cross conducted the Australian Covert Bullying Prevalence Study in 2009 and found that, 'Being bullied every few weeks or more often (considered to be frequent) overtly and/or covertly during the last term at school is a fairly common experience, affecting approximately one in four Year 4 to Year 9 Australian students (27%). Frequent school bullying was highest among Year 5 (32%) and Year 8 (29%) students'. The full document can be found at http://deewr.gov.au/bullying-research-projects#australiancovert-bullying-prevalence
2. An example of a definition of bullying can be found in the 2011 Australian National Safe Schools Framework Resource Manual: http://foi.deewr.gov.au/documents/national-safe-schools-framework-resource-manual
3. Professor Donna Cross conducted the Australian Covert Bullying Prevalence Study in 2009 and found that thirty-three per cent of boys and twenty-three per cent of girls experiencing bullying do not ask anyone for help. The full document can be found at http://deewr.gov.au/bullying-research-projects#australiancovert-bullying-prevalence
4. The 'map of the world' metaphor was first introduced in Alfred Korzybski's 1933 seminal work, *Science and Sanity: An Introduction to Non-Aristotelian Systems and General Semantics*.

5. A distinction we make in the field of Neuro-Semantics is that we have a mind–body–emotion system. This idea was first introduced by Alfred Korzybski in 1933.
6. 'Every and any emotion is always right. It is right given the map from which it comes' (Hall, *The Crucible*, 2010, page 57).
7. Robert Dilts makes clear, 'a belief does not have to be true to be believed' in his book, *Beliefs: Pathways to Health and Well-Being*, 1991 and 2012.
8. You can find the complete 'The Belief Change Pattern' in Dr L. Michael Hall's book *Secrets of Personal Mastery*, 2000, page 159.
9. The NLP Communication Model was first published in Richard Bandler and John Grinder's *The Structure of Magic*, Vol 1, 1975.
10. The Meta-Coach benchmarks were developed by Michelle Duval and Dr L. Michael Hall. You can find the listening benchmarks in *Meta-Coaching* Vol. 1, *Coaching Change*, 2004.
11. Dr L. Michael Hall documented fifteen different ways to respond to 'I don't know' in *Meta-Coach Reflections* #22, 1 June 2011. Find this article and more at www.neurosemantics.com
12. The distinction between self-esteem and self-confidence is explained fully in Dr L. Michael Hall's *The Crucible*, 2010, page 87.
13. Find the full version of the 'Meta-Stating Self Pattern' in Dr L. Michael Hall's book, *The Crucible*, 2010, page 91.
14. The four personal powers are listed in Dr L. Michael Hall's *Secrets of Personal Mastery*, 2000, page 64.
15. Read more about the distinction between what we are responsible *for* and who we are responsible *to* in Dr L. Michael Hall's *Secrets of Personal Mastery*, 2000, page 14.

16. You can find the full version Dr L. Michael Hall's Circle of Excellence Pattern in *The Sourcebook of Magic*, 2000, page 122.
17. Dr L. Michael Hall explores states in his book *Meta-States*, 2007.
18. Dr L. Michael Hall's Meta-Stating process can be found in *Secrets of Personal Mastery*, 2000, page 92.
19. Read more about emotions in Dr L. Michael Hall's book *Neuro-Semantics: Actualizing Meaning and Performance*, 2011, page 90.
20. While Dr L. Michael Hall wrote the book *Movie Mind*, the original source of that book was the *NLP Communication Model* (Bandler & Grinder). When asked, Michael humbly said he 'just added the movie metaphor'.
21. *'We have the unique and wonderful, and even magical, ability to literally re-present what we have experienced in our senses 'on the inside of our mind'* Dr L. Michael Hall's Movie Mind, 2003, page 22.
22. *'If you play a trauma scene (yours or someone else's) from within the movie as the key actor of the action, then you will experience more trauma'.* Dr L. Michael Hall's *Movie Mind* (page 61).
23. The idea of the Perceptual Positions was originated by Dilts, Grinder and DeLozier. Hall and Bodenhamer took what they developed and expanded it.
24. The 'changing the picture' approach is based on the NLP Communication Model by (Bandler & Grinder).
25. Perceptual flexibility exercise is based on the work by Judith DeLozier and Robert Dilts.
26. The Dutch social psychologist Lucas Derks first started using the term 'social panorama' in 1994.
27. Leslie Cameron Bandler developed the original ten Meta-Programs, Rodger Bailey developed and expanded them to fourteen in the LAB profile in Wyatt Woodsmall's

book *Time-Line Therapy* (1988). Dr L. Michael Hall and 'Bob' G. Bodenhamer expanded the Meta-Programs in their book *Figuring Out People: Design Engineering with Meta-Programs*, 2003. (Meta-Programs)
28. Cognitive distortions originally came from Aaron Beck and Albert Ellis, two key leaders in the field of Cognitive Psychology.
29. To find out more about cyberbullying visit the Australian Communications and Media Authority website at www.acma.gov.au or do a similar search in your country of residence.
30. For more information regarding bullies, do your own internet search using words such as 'bully', and 'bullying statistics' for examples of the information provided in Chapter Thirteen.

Bibliography and references

Bandler, Richard & Grinder, John (1975) *The Structure of Magic, Volume 1: A Book About Language and Therapy.* Palo Alto, CA: Science & Behavior Books.

Covey, Stephen. R (1989) The 7 Habits of Highly Effective People. United States, Free Press.

D. Cross, T. Shaw, L. Hearn, M. Epstein, H. Monks, L. Lester & L. Thomas (2009) Australian Covert Bullying Prevalence Study (ACBPS) research paper, Child Health Promotion Research Centre, Edith Cowan University, Perth.

Derks, Lucas (2005) *Social Panorama: Changing the Unconscious Landscape with NLP and Psychotherapy.* Cararthen, Wales: Crown House Publishing.

Hall, L. Michael (2011) *Neuro-Semantics: Actualizing Meaning and Performance.* Clifton, CO: Neuro-Semantic Publications.

Hall, L. Michael (2010) *The Crucible: And the Fires of Change.* Clifton, CO: Neuro-Semantic Publications.

Hall, L. Michael (2007) *Meta-States: Managing the Higher Levels of Your Mind's Reflexivity.* Clifton, CO: Neuro-Semantic Publications.

Hall, L. Michael (2006) *The Sourcebook of Magic: A Comprehensive Guide to NLP Change Patterns (2nd ed.)* Norwalk, CT: Crown House Publishing.

Hall, L. Michael (2003) *Movie Mind: Directing Your Mental Cinemas.* Clifton, CO: Neuro-Semantic Publications.

Hall, L. Michael (2000) *Secrets of Personal Mastery: Advanced Techniques for Accessing Your Higher Levels of Consciousness.* Wales, UK: Crown House Publishing.

Hall, L. Michael & Bodenhamer, Bob G. (2003) *Figuring Out People: Design Engineering with Meta-Programs.* Cararthen, Wales: Crown House Publishing.

Hall, L. Michael & Duval, Michelle (2004) *Meta-Coaching Volume 1: Coaching Change.* Clifton, CO: Neuro-Semantic Publications.

Hallbom, Tim & Smith, Suzi & Dilts, Robert (1991) *Beliefs: Pathways to Health and Well-being.* Portland, OR: Metamorphous Press.

Korzybski, Alfred (1933/1994) *Science and Sanity: An Introduction to Non-Aristotelian Systems and General Semantics* (5th ed.). Lakeville, CN: International Non-Aristotelian Library Publishing Co.

If you would like more information regarding Neuro-Semantics or Meta-Coaching, please visit the following websites: www.neurosemantics.com and www.metacoachfoundation.org

Index - Unbullyable

actions, power to choose 129–30
attitudes to bullying
    'character building' 14
Australian National Safe Schools Framework Resource Manual
    definition of bullying 20

behavioural strategies 15, 16, 66–7
    belief change and 71–73
behaviours
    signs of bullying 30–33
'The Belief Change Pattern' 57–61
    personal account 60–63
beliefs and meanings
    bullied children's beliefs 65–74
    changing 51–63,
    limiting 70–71
    parental 35–49
    power to choose 128
    relevance to bullying 22–3, 27–9
bullied children *see also* target of bullying
    beliefs and behavioural change 71–3
    changing beliefs, need for 70–1
    emotions 168–171
    influence of parents 67–8
    language, care with 68–9
    re-playing experiences 186
    thinking styles *see* thinking styles
    unresourceful beliefs 66
bullies 237–9, 249–251
    accountability 248
    common characteristics 243–4
    identification as 244–6
    interaction with target 25
    selection of targets 242–3
    self-awareness, lack of 246–7
    transformation, methods 247–9
    types 244–7
    why children bully 239–41
bullyable child 28, 134
bullying
    attitudes to 14
    components 20–2
    conversations about 75–96 *see also* communication

definitions 20–27, 33
impact 14–15, 46–8
intention of harm 20–1
meanings and beliefs 16–17, 22–3
rates of 13–14
self-esteem and *see* self-esteem
target of *see* target of bullying
unresourceful states 23–4
what is 19–27, 33
Circle of Excellence Pattern 135

communication 75–6, 95–6
    'annoying' advice 84–5
    benchmark guidance 85–6
    best state for 78–9, 154–5
    body language 80
    entering world of child 79–80
    feedback to child, giving 91–2
    'I don't know' responses 89–91
    listening 76–7, 83–6
    NLP communication model 78
    non-judgemental, remaining 86–7
    non-verbal rapport 81
    'pre-framing' conversation 83
    questions, using 87–9
    rapport, establishing 80–2
    sensory-based feedback 92–5
    verbal rapport 82
    what children want 76–7
    why questions, avoiding 88
Covey, Stephen
    Seven Habits of Highly Effective People 83
cyber safety 230–2
cyberbullying 221–22
    children's beliefs about 226–8
    effectiveness 224
    language of 228–30
    online safety 230–32
    other types of bullying, differences 223–5
    parents' beliefs about 225
    privacy 232–3
    Unbullyable approach 233–5
    what is 222–3

definitions of bullying 20–22, 33
    additional components 22–4
    children's definition 26–7
Dilts, Robert 53

INDEX

discounting 215–18
Duval, Michelle 85

emotions 178–9, 218–20
    awareness 167
    bullied child's 168–71
    child's beliefs about 166–7
    choosing 171–76
    containment 163–4
    duration, choosing 176
    empowering 157–79
    experience of 158, 163–6
    hiding 163
    intensity, choosing 173–6
    map of the world 167
    outbursts at home 32–3
    parents 40–4
    parents' beliefs about 162
    power to choose 128–9
    reality and 158–62
    response to child being bullied
        164
    support for child 176–8
    turning against oneself
        164
    type of, choosing 171–2
    what are 158–62
Empowering Students 52

feelings 23–4 *see also* emotions

Hall, Dr L. Michael 57, 85, 110,
    111, 126, 135, 147
    Movie Mind 189
harm, intention of 20–1, 24

listening to your child 76–7, 83–6

Meta-Coaching 9, 110
Meta-Stating Self Process 110, 113,
    122, 147
mind-body-emotion system 45
movies 181–83, 200–2
    acceptance of 190–1
    awareness of 190
    change of perspective
        191–93
    changing by child
        196–200
    characters 191
    creation of 182–6
    interpretation of events
        184
    parents' movies 193–4
    perceptual flexibility
        exercise 198–9
    picture, changing 196–8
    re-playing, effect 186–8,
        194–5
    re-presentation of bully
        195–6
    re-presentation of
        experiences 182

social panorama exercise 199–200
stepping out of 189–94, 196

Neuro-Linguistic Programming (NLP) 9, 77–8
Neuro-Semantics (NS) 9, 45, 99, 133

ongoing pattern of bullying 21, 24
online safety 230–2

parents
    awareness of meanings/beliefs/emotions 45–6, 48–9
    beliefs about bullying 38–40
    beliefs and meanings 35–49
    conditioning as child 38–9
    creation of beliefs 36–8
    cyberbullying beliefs 225
    emotional responses 40–44
    empowerment 54
    experience of being bullied as child 40, 46–8
    feelings of blame 15–16
    helping your child 45–6, 52
    influence on child's beliefs 67–8
    language, need for care with 68–9
    limiting or toxic beliefs 53–5
    map of the world 35–6, 51
    movies 193–4
    negative thinking 43
    positive thinking 43–4
    process for changing beliefs 57–63
    protectiveness 13
    resourceful or limiting beliefs, test of 55–7
    self-esteem 107–8
    states, child's experience of 152–3
    thoughts and beliefs, differences 52–3
    your rules 39–40
perceptual flexibility exercise 198–200
power 123, 139–40
    bullying and 125–6
    choices 122, 128–30
    language of 125–6
    ownership of personal powers 130–33, 138
    personal powers 126–30
    Power Zone process 135–7
    responsibility 134
    speech or silence, power of 130
power imbalance 22, 125, 139

powerlessness 125, 139
    child's feeling 15
    martyrdom 131
premeditation 21

relationships
    power imbalance 22
    relevance to bullying 21–2, 24
responsibility 133, 134 *see also* power

school, unwillingness to go 30–1
secrecy 29
self-confidence
    self-esteem and, difference 97–9
    what is 99–100, 120–21
self-esteem
    bullying and 106–7
    children 104–5, 114–20
    conditional 101–4, 105–6
    criteria 104–5
    devaluation of self 112–13
    explorative questions 116
    language 115–16, 120
    parents 107–9
    self-confidence and, difference 97–9
    self-esteeming process, step-by-step 109–12
    unconditional 100, 101–2, 105, 106, 108–9, 114, 121
    visualisation 116
    what is 100–1
sensory-based feedback 92–3
    example 93–5
sickness, increased 31–2
signs of being bullied 29–33
social isolation 31
social panorama exercise 199–200
states 155–6
    anchor 150–52
    awareness 142–3, 144–5, 148
    best state for communication 78–9, 154–5
    choice of *Unbullyable* state 148–9
    creation of 143
    examples of resourceful states 146–7
    experience of desired state 149
    importance within bullying experience 143–4
    intensity 150
    meaning of term 141–43
    parents' states, child's experience of 152–3
    resourceful 24
    Unbullyable, helping child create 144–52
    unresourceful 23–4, 145–6

statistics on bullying 13
strategies
    limited effectiveness where 15

target of bullying 14–15
    beliefs of 28, 65–74
    communication with 75–96
    interaction with bully 25
    selection by bully 242–3
thinking styles
    all-or-nothing thinking 206–10
    auditory processing 205
    bullying context 206
    discounting 215–18
    kinaesthetic processing 205
    language and 205–6
    over-generalising 213–15
    personalising 210–12
    processing information 204–6
    visual re-presentation 204–5
    what are 203–4
Unbullyable
    approach 15–17, 253–4
    child 28–9
    thinking styles 203–20

victims of bullying *see* bullied children; target of bullying

withdrawal of bullied child 31

Notes

About the author

Sue Anderson is a highly sought-after coach, trainer and presenter who coaches privately and within schools and organisations. She has a unique insight into how children and teenagers experience bullying and has worked with hundreds of primary school- and secondary school-aged children affected by bullying, including the targets, bullies, teachers and parents.

Sue grew up in Melbourne, Australia, as the youngest of five children. She travelled to the United States at age eighteen when she won a scholarship to attend university in Boise, Idaho, then returned to Australia to complete her degree at the University of Ballarat. She worked in the fitness, disability and quality assurance industries before gaining her international coaching qualifications in 2007, when she became a Meta-Coach.

Sue began using the cutting-edge methodology of Neuro-Semantics to coach children affected by bullying and was instantly astounded by the results. She has had great success empowering children and teenagers affected by bullying through her unique approach. With only word of mouth to promote them, Sue and her husband Chris Cartledge now run their successful coaching business, **Good2gr8 Coaching**.

Sue is an ambassador for Brodie's Law (the Victorian Anti Bullying legislation), a board member for the not-for-profit anti-bullying organisation Angel's Goal, and has a weekly radio segment on Ballarat's 3BA. She lives near Ballarat, in Victoria, with her husband and their three gorgeous children.

www.ingramcontent.com/pod-product-compliance
Lightning Source LLC
Chambersburg PA
CBHW050627300426
44112CB00012B/1697